Something To Think About!

Inspiring, encouraging and controversial stories

Edward Clark

Something To Think About!
Copyright © By Edward Clark
March 2020
All Rights Reserved.

This publication may not be reproduced, stored in a retrieval system or transmitted, in any form or in any means, in part or in whole, by electronic, mechanical, photocopying, recording or otherwise, without prior written permission of the author.

ISBN: 9781088796955

The Stanton Book Company
Palm Springs, California
www.stantonbooks.net

All scripture is derived from standard English versions of the Bible.

Printed in the United States of America

Meet Ed Clark & Family

Facebook: ed.clark.7

Ed Clark has worked in corporate America for nearly 30 years. During his tenure, he excelled in a variety of roles and responsibilities. The majority of his professional life was spent in the insurance and pharmaceutical industries. Ed Clark is a dynamic speaker who developed and delivered many presentations throughout the years. He holds two degrees; a Bachelor's Degree in Business Administration and Master's Degree in Organizational Leadership. In addition to his role as marketing representative for a major insurance company, he also teaches part-time at California State University Bakersfield. Married nearly 30 years, Ed and his wife have two adult children, one grandchild and, at this writing, are expecting their second grandchild.

Although many of those who inspired me have passed away, the knowledge and passion I display comes from their positive attitudes despite challenging situations. My wife, Annabelle, and two children, Alexis Maynor and Isaac Clark, have been consistent sources of encouragement and often the reasons that I write. I also want to thank the many friends who offered words of encouragement during this process. I would never have thought about writing a book had it not been for those who believed in me before I believed in myself.

"I can do all things through Christ who strengthens me."

Philippians 4:13

Are You Too Busy?

I was reading a post today about someone who lost a loved one and it got me to thinking about the fact that our words don't always match our actions. We say we appreciate friends and family and yet we don't take time to show it with our actions. I often hear things like: I wish I would have spent more time and did more things with so-and-so, but I was too busy. I am convinced that BUSY is a four-letter word that means someone or something is not a priority. Busy is the catch-all for everything that we don't want to do. I amaze myself with how BUSY I am when it comes to reading a good book, but never too busy to watch TV. I find it hard to get to the gym, but it's never too hard for me to eat a double cheeseburger. I am going to challenge myself to 'get busy' doing the things in life that need to be done, and to be less busy with the things that aren't important.

The Cup That Saved Me!

After reading many stories about Starbucks and Duncan Donuts and their cup designs, I find it very interesting that the internet and politicians all have something to say about a disposable cup. In a country where we have many issues to deal with such as homelessness, unemployment, poverty, sickness, disease and a multitude of other issues, we're sure are spending a lot of time talking about something that will be used for one minute and then discarded. For those Christians who want to boycott Starbucks because of their 'seasonal cup design' I want you to ask yourself, why you go there in the first place. If your new, favorite place is now Duncan Donuts because of their new, SEASONAL cups, I have the same question. If you only support a business because of their social values, then you need to ask yourself what values are important to you, because you'll find yourself not supporting a ton of businesses that aren't considered "CHRISTIAN". In my world, the cup that saved me was filled with the blood of a person who loved me, despite who I was! And now, it's about what I am and what I can do for him; and the best thing about that cup is, it was free and I didn't have to wait in line to get it. All I had to do was ask for it!

Completion

It is finished! Throughout the years I've had an opportunity to see my son, Isaac Clark, do a lot of things. I've watched him compete at the highest level of every sport he participated in. I've been present at numerous award ceremonies and even had the opportunity to coach him in a variety of sports! Although all these things were great, they paled in comparison to watching him walk across the stage to receive his Bachelor's Degree! The only words I can say are: I'm so thankful and proud of you for finishing this part of the journey! Although he did the work, he had a great support system to guide him, and I really appreciate all of them! Congratulating to my son, Isaac Clark!

Loneliness

Social media has a way of bringing up topics that need to be addressed, but aren't always discussed. Recently, I read a post about 'loneliness' that was heartbreaking. This topic hit me hard because it was all too real, and the comments on the thread helped me realize that this phenomenon impacts more people than we may be aware of. In a world with billions of people, you would think that everyone might have some friends they can count on to be there for them. Sadly, this issue isn't limited to one particular segment of society; it's even happening in churches! As a society we've become so focused on our own needs, that we have forgotten about others. When God created Adam, he said, "It is not good for man to be alone." Although Adam's need was different, the premise of companionship is the same. We need one another! Unless a person wants to be alone, there is no excuse for people being lonely. As a society, we need to put down our toys, break up our cliques and get out of our comfort zones! People need the warm energy that is only provided by human interaction. Unfortunately, some people won't initiate gatherings due to pride or fear. However, I believe that when we let go of such hindrances, we'll find that 'people interaction' is a positive for us all. And, as we engage in human interaction, we'll find that we'll all be happier as a society. Please join me in breaking up loneliness!

Politics

Although I don't talk about politics often, I would like to share something from my heart. For the last 10 years, I read and listened to the people in this country bash the president. It started with President Obama and is continuing with President Trump. I am sure that there is justification in the minds of those doing the bashing. However, my question is this: what's the point in bashing them? I'm sure that most of us were taught that if we can't say anything nice about someone, then we shouldn't say anything at all. Neither side wants to acknowledge the good that either president has accomplished. Yet the bad, or should I say the stuff that people don't agree with, is mentioned on a daily basis. All presidents have flaws because they are human and there are many things I don't agree with from any president. However, I don't feel it's necessary to complain about something that I can't do anything about. As a Christian, the Bible tells me that I must pray for my leaders! It doesn't tell me to just pray for those I agree with. I will not unfriend, dislike or argue with anyone who thinks differently than myself, nor will I try to change the opinion of anyone else. I only ask this: if you are a person of prayer, please join me in praying for the leadership of this country. Regardless of your point of view, prayer will change more things than complaining on social media.

Christianity

The biggest problem the world has with Christianity is Christians--not Christ! Many people say they won't go to church because the church is full of hypocrites. I must admit that I agree with that statement. However, my point of view is a little different. When sick people go to the doctor, they're supposed to get better. The same is true for Christians going to church; they should be better and act better as a result of attending church. The problem many people have with Christians is that they don't see change from people who go to church every week. I'm not saying that Christians are supposed to be perfect! However, I am saying that a person who calls themselves a Christian should and act differently from the world. The Bible says that we all fall short and need the grace of God to make it to heaven. Just because it's understood that Christians will fall short, is no reason for Christians to live a life that hurts God's reputation! If we claim to be Christians and we walk around with hate in our hearts, then we aren't representing Christ! If we choose to condemn those that are different, instead of loving them, are we showing the love of God to the world? Somehow, this "love only people like us" mentality has crept into the church. If we really want to see change in others, then I feel that this change starts with us! Let's start living and loving like Christ, and see how many others will be attracted to him and us!

Something To Think About For Men:

She Needs Your Arm More Than Your Hand

While on vacation the other day, my wife and I were walking around holding hands, looking like lost tourists. Out of the blue, she said that she preferred to hold my arm, instead of my hand. This is not an unusual occurrence due to our height discrepancy. However, this time I decided to ask why. And she calmly said, "It's because your arm is closer to my heart." Her statement made me think, and I realized a simple truth. What's most important to our spouses is to be close to their hearts at all times. Here's a term to consider... "keeping someone at arm's length" ... which means: keeping a distance from something or someone to avoid intimacy or familiarity. My wife's simple statement made me realize that I often, like many others, have kept my spouse at my hand, which is the furthest distance from my body, instead of my arm, which is closest to my heart! Men, let's try to do a better job of holding our wives close to our hearts, instead of at arm's length!

Peaceful Protests

I've watched and listened to people complain about peaceful protests over the last year. The main argument I heard is that, it's disrespectful to the military, and to those who fought and died for our country. I have yet to hear anyone say when and where it's okay to protest. I would like to share a different perspective and would like to hear back from you. First of all, let's keep in mind that all major changes in society started with a protest. The Revolutionary War, the Civil war, Women's Suffrage and the Civil Rights Movement, just to name a few, all got started as a result of a protest. Many lives were lost in the pursuit of a cause and subsequent better treatment. The problem with using the "disrespecting the military argument" is this: the brave men and women who fought, and in some cases died for our country, were fighting for our rights. Those rights included the right to protest. In many other countries, people would be killed for protesting, yet our country allows such things. It could be argued that, those who oppose people exercising their right to protest, are being just as disrespectful to the military. Who gets to choose what rights are exercised? Whether you agree or disagree with the cause, I feel that it's better to support a peaceful protest, even if you are silent, than to complain about a person's rights. When the Montgomery bus boycott was announced, the bus companies became upset. Many people resorted to violence to show their displeasure. Many lives were lost during that time period, and injustice was rampant. So, please share when and how a person is supposed to get their points across-- if not by protesting.

Memorial Day

As I was thinking about Memorial Day celebrations, it occurred to me that we're celebrating those who made the ultimate sacrifice for our country. No matter what is posted or written, those who passed away will never see it. So, it got me to thinking that, I/we need to say 'thank you' to the families of those brave men and women who gave their all for me/us. I've also come to the conclusion that we need to take time to appreciate those who serve and have served, whenever the opportunity arises, since we never know when they will be called into duty, to protect us. And, we may not get a chance later. So, please join me in thanking THE FAMILIES of those who died for our freedom. I also want to thank those who serve now, have served and will serve in the future, because without your willingness to sacrifice, I wouldn't have the opportunities I have today!

Opportunity

Like many others when I graduated from college, I was done with school! I had no desire to be affiliated with the school as an alumni because I felt that college had served its purpose. I had a job that required a degree and was working in Corporate America. However, in 2017, I received an email from my old university that piqued my interest. I was invited to an alumni mixer, and I went. What I saw at the event, rekindled my fire for my school. When I saw the impact that National University, my alma mater, was having in the community, I was filled with pride and overwhelmed with joy! The impact the graduates had in the fields of education and nursing blew me away! After the event, I made a point to get involved so that I too could be a difference-maker. I joined the local alumni chapter, whereupon I've had the opportunity to impact my local area. As many of you know, I was given the opportunity to speak at the Northern California Commencement last week. It was an awesome opportunity and a great experience!

Progress

On this date, 55 years ago, Dr. Martin Luther King, Jr. and Robert Kennedy were on hand to witness the signing of the Civil Rights Act. It could be argued that this signing was the most significant event to address race relations since the Emancipation Proclamation. Some will say that change has been slow, and race relations are no different than they were 55 years ago, while others will say that we're doing a good job in the area of race relations. Both sides can be debated and there would be no clear winner. The reality is that, we are closer to Dr. King's dream than we were 55 years ago. Although we should be hopeful that we can live in a world where everyone is treated equally, we'd be very naïve to expect 100 percent participation, since there will always be fools amongst us. We'd also be extremely blind and unaware if we can't see that we aren't in a better world today, than were 55 years ago. Change will only come when people decide to work together for a common goal. 55 years ago, we saw a rainbow of people stand together for a common cause. Let's see what we can do today with all this technology, and continue to make the world a better place!

Independence Day

On the 4th of July, 1776, several imperfect men declared their independence from Great Britain. Their vision for a better country with less taxes and equal rights for all was noble, but flawed. However, their vision has allowed many people to achieve dreams and goals that wouldn't have been possible, had they stayed chained to Britain. Sadly, their vision of equality was flawed, partly because their vision only involved people who were from Britain and looked like they did. Progress to incorporate others was slower than it should have been, and it could be argued that we still aren't there yet. However, the freedoms that we enjoy in America are envied by many from around the world! The United States of America will never be perfect! However, if we as a country desire progress and equality for all, then we'll be able to overcome the imperfections of our forefathers' vision!

The "Other" Independence Day

In a few days, our wonderful country will be celebrating the Declaration of Independence; also known as The 4th of July, the date that we formally declared our independence from England. Although I'm a proud American, I feel that I must share about the "Other Independence Day" so that others can become informed about OUR history. Although the United States of America declared their independence on the 4th of July, 1776, many African Americans didn't gain their independence until June 19th 1865. President Abraham Lincoln issued the Emancipation Proclamation on September 22, 1862, with an effective date of January 1, 1863. Sadly, many Blacks were not aware of the Emancipation Proclamation until June 19, 1865. Due to a lack of teaching in schools and in many families, this date hasn't been discussed as much as it should. June 19, 1865 is just as significant to the African American Community as Cinco de Mayo is to Hispanics, or any other cultural celebration. Many communities hold celebrations to commemorate this date. If we as a country, truly want unity, we must make sure that we teach our children and grandchildren the importance of June 19, 1865, as fervently as we teach about the 4th of July. African American history is also American history. Let's become culturally aware so that we can become better informed people.

Which Past?

Lately, I've been doing a lot of thinking about things that occurred in the past. Often times, people say, "Forget the past because you can't do anything about it." Although I agree with this theory wholeheartedly, I'd like to share a different point of view. No one's "past" is all good or all bad. If you learned from your mistakes, then it wasn't a mistake--it was a lesson! If we forget about our past, then we could be ignoring those valuable lessons in life that made us who we are today! Your past can be your teacher or your torturer. The choice is yours. Choose your past memories wisely.

Christians and Politics

Although I know this is a touchy subject, I'm trying to figure out what the Christian political party is in America. Is there even a Christian party? Fact: at this writing, the current president, Donald J. Trump, is supported by many Christians because he is pro-life. However, Trump is also hated by many Christians because he's called a racist and doesn't know when to stop talking. The previous president, Barack Obama, was supported by many Christians because he was classy and a good family man; although he was a very strong supporter of abortion. He was hated by many because of his race and some of his policies. Interestingly enough, both presidents have done some of the same missteps while in office. However, their missteps are only reported by the other party when it's convenient. Now, back to my question: who is the Christian party? What defines a Christian leader? If both parties are defining themselves as Christians, what criteria are they using? And finally, what behaviors should be displayed by Christians when 'the other party' is in office? Should they pray for their leaders like the Bible instructs? Or, should they condemn and ridicule the person in authority? Is a person more of a Christian because they are a Republican or a Democrat? Think on these things.

Aging Parents

Since I was able to visit my 86-year old dad today, I've been doing a lot of thinking about the aging process. Additionally, many of my friends have either lost parents recently, or they're seeing their parent's age right before their eyes. Although I'm not an expert on aging or the stages that are associated with it, I thought I would share some thoughts. Death and aging are the motions of life that no one wants to talk about. However, avoiding the topic isn't going to change the inevitable. First of all, I suggest that you cherish every moment you have with your parents and grandparents. Take notes about special moments and take plenty of pictures so that you'll remember the events. Be patient with them. Many of them are struggling with the fact that they aren't able to do what they used to. Try to be understanding. Our family members are aware of the fact that they have fewer days left, and some of them are afraid of dying. Most of all, I recommend that you love them and give them plenty of time and affection. They may say things that you aren't expecting, and they may come across as mean. Don't hold onto the negative. When things get tough, understand that it's just a part of life. Lastly, I recommend joining a support group. Watching a parent struggle is not easy. But you must understand that you're not alone. Talk to your friends and family or a professional if necessary. Just don't suffer in silence.

Are You Sabotaging Your Happiness?

A few weeks ago, someone asked me a certain question which has bothered me ever since. After thinking about the question for the last month or so, I want to share some thoughts about it. First of all, I must admit that the question bothered me because of the truth it spoke to me. Personally speaking, I realized that my usual high, and sometimes unrealistic expectations of myself and others, causes me to be disappointed. In effect, transferring the shortcomings of others over my life, has caused me to be frustrated. This is an improper balance in life. An improper life-balance can lead to emotional shortcomings that eventually manifest as depression, anxiety and other mental issues. One way to achieve happiness is to look at things with the right perspective, and to have a grateful heart. Hating on another person and their success isn't going to make your life any better. Also, not recognizing your own blessings is a cause of concern. If you can't appreciate what you have now, what makes you think you'll appreciate having more? The bottom line in life is this: learn to be thankful and happy for who you are and what you have! Then, you won't be a person sabotaging their own happiness.

Life's Not Fair

I was reading an article the other day that mentioned how some words and phrases are no longer used. As I looked at some of the phrases, I started thinking about a phrase I believed everyone was using, which is, "THAT'S NOT FAIR!" After pondering that phrase a little bit more, I realized there is a very famous person who never used that phrase. That person was JESUS! He took a beating and died for us all, and instead of saying, "Father, this isn't fair," he asked his father to forgive us. If that isn't love, then I don't know what love is. The moral of the story is this: when we think life isn't treating us fairly, we need to remember the cross. Jesus was treated unfairly so that we could have a fair life, and an opportunity to live with him forever!

Forgiveness

I am convinced that the Lord speaks to me about something and then he allows me to share my shortcomings with the world. I had an opportunity to teach Sunday school this morning and I felt that I needed to share about forgiveness. The sad reality is that Christians struggle in this area just like non-Christians. The bottom line is that forgiveness is a choice! Holding a grudge against someone else doesn't hurt them, it only hurts the person holding the grudge. Forgiving is not about forgetting; it's about letting go and letting God deal with the situation. We all fall short and we all need forgiveness. The next time that you're thinking about not forgiving a person, ask yourself if you would want someone to forgive you--if you wronged them.

Jackie Robinson

On April 15, 1947, American sports were changed forever when Jackie Robinson made his major league debut for the Brooklyn Dodgers. Historians will tell the story of his accolades on the baseball field. However, I want to take a moment and share a little about his accomplishments as a person. Most people don't realize that Jackie Robinson was the first person to 'letter' in four sports at UCLA. He lettered in football, basketball, baseball and track. In addition to his college sports accolades, he was a great tennis player too, who won a high-level, all-Black tournament after high school. As impressive as Jackie was as an athlete, his character was even more impressive, which is why he was chosen as the first Black person to play in the major leagues. He was a second lieutenant in the army, then a sports commentator, a company executive and a civil rights activist. Although Jackie Robinson will always be remembered for what he did on the baseball field, let's not forget what he did for our society! Without the contributions of people like Jackie Roosevelt Robinson, we would not be enjoying the civil rights advances we currently enjoy. Sports is never just a game. They are also vehicles of change.

I Wish…

I was just thinking how I oftentimes hear people say they wish they'd done this or that in their lives. After doing much reflection about this issue in my own life, I realized that oftentimes I forget that God is in control! The many things I may have wanted to do, may have led me down a path away from his desired will for my life. I firmly believe that God wants to bless us immensely and give us our hearts' desires. Sometimes, however, our hearts become corrupted, whereupon God may have to take something away from us, in order to refocus and live for him! God's love for us is the ultimate example of tough love. So, the next time you're not going where you ought to go, I suggest that you ask God for his direction. I'm confident that he'll order your footsteps!

Dr. Martin Luther King, Jr.

On January 15, 1929 Dr. Martin Luther King, Jr. was born. It can be argued that Dr. King was one of the most influential leaders of 20th century. Although, his flaws have been well documented, and he was very controversial. However, I strongly believe that his influence has and will span generations. As discussed earlier, some people will say that his purpose was making things better for Black Americans. However, if take the time to understand his mission, you'll see that his PURPOSE was to make things better for **all people**. His leadership galvanized people from all walks of life, all races and ethnicities to achieve his goals. He dreamed so that we could dream. We can't minimize where we are today and should never forget where we came from. Thank you, Dr. King, for your dream, your passion, your life and sacrifice! I am proof that his dream is alive and progressing. And I plan to do everything I can to keep progress moving forward!

Impact

This small, six-letter word...impact...can have various meanings, depending on your perspective. Everyone's life has been impacted by someone else. Some impacts are positive, while some are negative. A challenging childhood caused me to see the negative impact of others for many years. Junior high was really challenging because I found myself at a predominantly white school during the height of the Civil Rights Movement. Name calling and verbal abuse were rampant back in the day, and some teachers were just as bad as some of the students. Sports, in particular basketball, was my saving grace. Although I wasn't any good, I met another kid who was really good. It turns out that he and his family took me under their wings. Although I didn't achieve all my basketball goals, the impact that this family had on my life was far more valuable than just basketball. They loved me for who I was. They prayed for me and their influence positively impacted my family as well! Their impact on me is one of the reasons that I try to help others. We never know what impact we will have on another person until we take time to get to know them.

Investment

When we hear the word 'investment' it's oftentimes associated with money. However, I want share some thoughts about the most important investment a person can make, and that is the investment of 'time.' As I reflect back over this past weekend, I can only think of one thing, and that is how blessed I am! Although I may not be the richest or wisest person in the world, I am one of the most blessed, because my investment in people always seems to manifest itself at the right time. Regardless of the situation, the people I invested my time in have always made time for me when I needed it the most. Take for instance my daughter's wedding. I was grateful to those who attended her wedding, for their 'investment' in her, as she began her new life. I was also grateful to the pastors, teachers and leaders in her life who constantly prayed for her--also an investment in her life. Since time is a limited resource, we must use it wisely if we want to get the best return. Thank you all for a great return on my investment!

Brokenness

A word like brokenness isn't usually associated with good times. Usually, a broken person is one who is at the end of their rope. Brokenness is one step away from hopelessness. However, brokenness in the sight of God is the place where God can do the most for you. When a person comes to the realization that they can't deal with life issues alone, God is able to step in and help them, right where they are. Too often, pride and arrogance keep people from asking for help, and as a result of not seeking help, they'll continue the vicious cycle that caused the problems in the first place. I can testify to the fact that when I surrender my will to God, great things begin to happen! Sometimes, that great thing is having peace in my life. Recently, a friend told me that their life turned around completely during a broken stage. They said they simply quit trying to do everything on their own and gave it all to God. Although they didn't know what God was going to do, they knew that it was better than what they were dealing with all alone. The reality is this: as people, we can only do so much, but God is able to do exceedingly more than we can ask or hope for. My suggestion is to change your attitude before it breaks you. However, if you do fall into brokenness, know that there is still hope for you in God.

Compassion

With graduation and wedding obligations these past few weeks, a thought was constantly on my mind, which I feel the need to share. It seems to me that as a society we've become so caught up in our own personal issues, that we've forgotten that the world doesn't revolve around us. Many people believe that they have compassion if they take a moment to flash a smile or leave a tip in the tip jar at their favorite establishment. But the reality is that we've become so callused toward people that we rarely show compassion toward anyone. Our society has morphed into a place that says, "If it doesn't impact me, I don't care." There are a variety of reasons why this sentiment has become more prevalent. Although there are a lot of reasons why we have turned a deaf ear toward others, the reality is that none of them are good reasons. As human beings, we need to treat others as we would want to be treated. Compassion doesn't always mean giving money. Compassion does mean giving time and attention to causes that aren't necessary about us. How much more progress could we have if we decide to investigate issues and stand with those that have been mistreated or have a need? When I think of the great leaders of the past, I'm reminded of how they took stands that served the greater good, not just themselves. Let us all start thinking like them and see what we can do as a unified group of people who shows compassion for their fellow human beings!

Accomplishments

Over the last few weeks I observed a mentality that is very concerning, and sadly self-perpetuated. As a result of this thinking, I feel that I need to share a point of view. I've seen and heard about people graduating from various schools at various levels, losing weight, starting new jobs and a variety of other things. I personally believe that all these events are great accomplishments! However, it appears that the people accomplishing these goals are minimizing their importance, because they may not be as "grand" as someone else. Webster's dictionary defines the word 'accomplishment' as: "the act of completing something." Nowhere in the definition does it say that your accomplishment is minimized because it was different than someone else's. I believe that people would be a lot happier once they start appreciating what they accomplished personally, versus comparing their achievements to others. Keep in mind also that, what may seem small to you, is very large to someone else!

Hurdles

As I was watching the hurdle races at a track meet the other day, I was reminded of how this race is a great symbol of life. Everyone has hurdles in life, some have high hurdles while others have low ones. I saw some people hit their hurdles and fall down and not get up due to injury, while others who hit a hurdle fell down, got back up and finished. Still others hit some hurdles, but finished strong. I think we can learn from all the athletes described here, since we will go through all these periods in life. Remember also that the race is not always won by the swift or the strong, but by those that ENDURE to the end. Keep in mind that no matter what hurdle in life you are facing, you will decide how you get through it.

Parenting - Part 1

Communication.

Communication is key in all relationships. However, when it comes to parenting, there is nothing more important than a parent's ability to communicate with their child/children. Sadly, many people believe that communication is defined as 'talking.' Although we need to use words to get our points across, it's important to note that communication isn't just what is being said. True communication is what is being heard and understood by the child and the parent. In some households you would think that the families are speaking two different languages, since there is no true communication! As a parent, we must learn to understand how our child/children receives from us. Keep in mind that one child may receive differently than another one. I have learned from experience that I can have the same discussions with my kids and they both come out with a different understanding of what I said and meant. As a parent, I must do my best to understand their words and encourage them to do a good job of explaining their sides, so that we can have better communication. There is no one way to communicate. The best way to communicate is the one that yields the best results in your family!

Parenting Part - 2

Time.

I must admit that the issue of time has been the biggest challenge for me that I've had to deal with. As a child, I felt that I wasn't given enough time for the important things in my life and, as a parent, I've often struggled with making sure I have the time boundaries necessary for everyone in my family. My childhood challenge lies around the fact that, as a child, I was ignorant and a bit selfish. Ignorant in the sense that I didn't know or understand the immense pressure my dad was under, trying to raise two children after my mother passed away. He often worked two jobs and sometimes three, to make ends meet. The selfishness came from seeing my friends with their parents at games and there was no one there for me. As an adult I was determined to be involved in my children's lives and participate in their activities, regardless of the time commitment. Although this was a noble idea, it became emotionally debilitating because I realized that I couldn't be everywhere at once. As a parent, it's important to realize that although you desire to spend a lot of time with your children, you must maintain a balance, and set your priorities in order. Work and other family obligations must be factored into the equation. No parent should feel guilty about missing an activity because they had to provide for their family by working. A smart parent will prioritize and make sure they are at the events that are most important to the child. A smart parent will also communicate with their children about the reasons why they can't attend everything. Understanding the value of time will make you and your family's lives much better.

Friends

This is a message I believe is important to discuss at the beginning our children's school year. Can we pray for the kids that have trouble making friends? They are people just like us who need friends. Can we also pray that the bullying should STOP? NO ONE deserves to be mistreated, regardless of how they look, dress or act. We are different for a reason and our differences are what make us special. If everyone were the same, this world would be pretty boring. Can we also pray for the parents of those children, since I'm sure it's very hard for them to see their children suffer? Thanks for your support! I believe that we can make a difference if we unify!

What's Next?

I've noticed that many of my friends are transitioning into empty nests. Many of them were active in their children's lives and gave many years to their kids' activities and events. As a result of this change, many of us are wondering what's next for us. I would like to share some thoughts on this. First of all, keep in mind that you were blessed to be part of your children's lives. However, their life is theirs and your life is yours. Just because your child is no longer in the house doesn't mean your value to society has diminished. Do you have a dream that you put on hold while raising your children? If so, start chasing it again. Refuel your passion! Rekindle your relationship with your spouse. Start dating again! Remember that our children are an addition to our lives, not our whole lives. Don't be afraid to enjoy life just because they are gone. If you were a good parent, then your kids will be happy that you are happy.

Dear Fear...

Fear, I wanted to let you know that I am done with you! When I was younger, you caused me to make some bad decisions and, as I got older, you became controlling and abusive! You made me stay home for college because I was afraid of what could have happened to me had I left! You made me choose the wrong college because I was afraid that I wasn't smart enough to go to another one! You made me stay at a job I didn't like because you told me there was nothing better for me! You made me stay quiet in bad relationships because I was afraid to take a stand! Fear, you controlled so many areas of my life that I feel I wasn't living life at all! I was just passing through! Well, today I am declaring my independence from you! I will no longer be burdened by your mean, lying and hateful ways! From this day forward, I plan to live life to the fullest and you will no longer be a part of it!

Goodbye forever!

Failure

The other day I was thinking about how many times I failed, and how many things I failed at. Here's my short version:

I failed at being a husband!
  I failed at being a dad!
    I failed at being a son!
      I failed at being an uncle!
        I failed at being a brother!
          I failed at being a friend!
            I failed as an employee!

My list of failures is too long to write and too depressing to think about. As a matter of fact, I probably failed at just about everything I ever tried in my life! In the past, my failings really got to me (I'm not saying they don't bother me now), and then I realized a simple truth: Failure is an EVENT--not a person! People fail because at least they're trying! Parents don't get upset when they see their child fall down, after taking his first few steps! Likewise, we should not beat ourselves up for failing when we're trying to improve ourselves. Our failures should not be an indictment of who we are! Instead, our failures should be considered honorable battle scars, for who and what we are trying to become! I will leave you with this thought: you will never be great if you are afraid to fail!

Count Your Blessings

I felt a need to share this thought with those of you who may have had a bad day. When you're feeling down, start counting your blessings. Start by looking in the mirror. If you can see yourself, then you have something to be thankful for. If you can stand on your own two healthy legs, then you have something else to be thankful for. If you can brush your teeth and comb your hair, then you have something to be thankful for. If you have food to eat, then you have something to be thankful for. If you have the ability to read this, then you have something to be thankful for. I am sure that you get the point. When things are bad we still have a lot to be thankful for.

God's Best

As I sit here today, I realize that my mind sometimes keeps me from receiving the best from God! Too often, I find myself questioning him instead of trusting him for his guidance! God has the best track record in history. He has never failed anyone and, despite how he has been treated, he is constantly reaching out to us! If we, as a human race, had even one percent of the love for others that God has for us, then we could turn this world around! Please join me in trying to be more like him so that we can turn the world right-side up!

Who Are You Listening To?

What does a former pastor, cruise friend and one of my college students have in common? They were the instruments that God used to encourage me recently. In today's world, we are inundated with negative news and opinions. If a person isn't careful, they can get caught up and start acting like their negative environment. Due to a variety of things I've been dealing with lately, I found myself getting caught up in a web of negativity. When I realized what was happening to me, I changed who I listened to. All three of these people had the perfect word for me at the right time. Interestingly enough, these people have known me for different time periods and in different capacities. Yet, their words were right on point. My point is this: when you find yourself being overwhelmed with life, ask yourself, "Who are you listening to?"

Voting and Politics

I thought I'd share some thoughts with you about the 2018 mid-term election process, specifically, a certain perspective about Christians and politics. As I mature, I realize that politics will always be a hot button issue in our society. However, just because it's a hot button, doesn't mean Christians should not be involved in the political process! I will never ever tell anyone how they should vote! However, I will say that we need to educate ourselves about the issues, so that we can make informed decisions. I will also say that we need to do a better job of following the scriptures when it comes to dealing with our leaders. As Christians, we are not required to like or agree with our leaders (including our bosses). 1st Timothy 2: 1-3 tells us that we need to pray for our leaders. Proverbs 18:21 tells us that our tongue has the power of life and death. Let's try to do a better a job of using our tongues to pray for those officials over us, instead of bashing them.

It's All About the Dash
Part 1

Regardless of how long a person lives, there will be a dash between our dates of birth and our dates of death. Although I am confident that most people want a long gap between the years, I am thoroughly convinced that the most import part of life is what you do in between the dashes--the years! We all have a limited amount of time on this Earth. However, those people who choose to make a difference will be remembered. Your dash doesn't have to involve money or fame. If lives are positively impacted because of your existence, then your dash will be remembered. The Bible tells me that a good name is more desirable than riches. My goal is to make a difference in the lives of those I interact with. Whether it be personally, professionally or digitally. I plan to make a difference. Please join me in focusing on your dash.

It's All About the Dash
Part 2

Death is the part of life that no one wants to talk about, and it's also the part of life that is the most difficult to deal with. Over the last couple of months, several of my family members and friends pass away. Although I was saddened by their passing, I rejoiced in the fact that 'their dash' left me with a lot of great memories! Death is going to happen to everyone. However, it's our responsibility to make sure that we impact the world in a way that people will have fond memories about our dash! It's never too late to make a difference, so let's start 'doing different' today!

The Vacation Journey

The last few days have been interesting for me because I dealt with a variety of emotions. due to things going on in my world. When I'm going through a challenging time I like to reflect on the blessings and positive things that have happened in my life. Today's thought was around vacation. I LOVE being on vacation, but I hate 'the journey' to the vacation! After some more reflection, I started thinking that I seem to have the concept of vacation twisted; just like many people have the concept of life twisted. We want to be seen on vacation and not on the journey. To properly plan a vacation, you need to plan. The plan must be detailed and will most likely contain some things that aren't pleasant. During the planning phase, you will have to be disciplined; you will have be focused and you need to keep your eyes on the goal. Finally, when you arrive at the destination, you'll take a ton of photos and show all your friends and family. You're happy and your friends are happy for you! The problem with this picture is that--everyone sees the end result but not the journey. I believe that if you want to impact lives, share with them your entire journey! Some of life's most important lessons are learned 'on the way' to the destination!

Faith vs. Fear

While I was having a conversation the other day, the topic of faith versus fear came up. I know many people struggle with FAITH and fear, myself included. So, I thought I'd share a quick thought on this topic. Faith isn't simple! It takes believing in something that we can't see and sometimes even imagine. The interesting thing is, fear is the same thing in reverse. If you look at the spelling of fear it says...

        F   FALSE
        E   EXPECTATIONS
        A   APPEARING
        R   REAL!!

So, which person do you want to be? The faith-filled person or the fear-filled person? I choose faith because

BELIEVING GOD IS A LOT BETTER THAN WALKING IN FEAR!

Let It Go!

This is a true story and proves that God has a sense of humor. One Saturday, I prayed that my focus would be to 'love people' exactly where they are, despite who they are. Within 24 hours, I was face to face with a person that I was no fan of, for a variety of reasons. But, I was inside a store and didn't have time to escape to another aisle. I was forced to engage with that person. Interestingly, my pastor preached about allowing God to vindicate us and to let things go the week before. Needless to say, I'm doing a better job today, of letting things go, because I don't desire for God to put me in those awkward positions again, in order to teach me something I should already know. I hope you enjoyed this story!

Why Should I Care?

"Why do you care? It's my life! I'll be fine!" For the large majority of my adult life, I've heard people say these things to me, while I was trying to help them with whatever situation they may have been going through. This past summer while I was trying to help an ungrateful friend find a job, it finally hit me. Why do I actually care? It's their life, after all. The lesson I learned that day was simple, yet profound. I don't need to care! However, I do need to have compassion. Not everyone needs my or anyone else's help. But when a person comes to me, then I should have compassion and be prepared to help. I must admit that this new perspective has been liberating and also gratifying! The moral of the story is simple: have compassion for those who desire your help, and don't waste your time worrying about people who don't want to be helped! After all, it's their life!

Veterans' Day

When I think about Veterans' Day, I can't help but think about Memorial Day as well. The two holidays are celebrated 6 months apart, which is a reminder to me of the importance of our military. I truly believe that these days should be called 'Freedom Days.' Freedom of Speech, Freedom of Religion, Freedom to Protest and the many other freedoms afforded to us a nation, because of the sacrifices of the men and women who chose to put their lives on the line, ahead of themselves. Our veterans deserve their day in the sun because many times they worked in the night to protect us. Please join me in honoring those men and women who serve now, and served in the past, by wishing them a Happy Veterans' Day!

Choices

While driving in my car the other day, I started thinking about my life and how my choices have shaped where I am, and where I could have been. Not all my choices have been good or bad. As a matter of fact, a good choice may not have been the best choice, and a bad choice could have been worse at the time. As a result, of this conversation with myself, I made a promise to myself to try and make the best choices possible, at all times. Here's a small list of choices I will start and/or continue. Hopefully you will join me!

I choose to love and not hate
I choose to pray and not worry
I choose to listen more and talk less
I choose to engage in more dialogue and less debate
I choose to appreciate what I have and not complain about what *I don't have*
I choose to apologize more and argue less
I choose to accept others and judge less
I choose to encourage others more and discourage less
I choose to give more and take less
Please try these few things and see what a difference 'choices' can make!

Are You Really Thankful?

As I reflect on the Thanksgiving weekend, I realized that my actions don't always reflect true thanksgiving. The last few days have really helped me put things in perspective. The other day, I sent a friend a birthday text, and as we were chatting, they told me that they were diagnosed with a rare disease and they were only given a year or two to live. Another person shared with me that they were diagnosed with MS, and that person is only in their early 30's. After having those two conversations, I realized that a thankful life should be lived more than spoken, and that a thankful life should be on display year-round, not just one day or one month of the year. Often times we, as people, get so used to having ALL our blessings, that we forget what it's really like to be thankful. Both these people inspired me to have and attitude of gratitude, regardless of my situation. I am challenging anyone who reads this to start cultivating a thankful attitude at all times, not just when things are going well. Remember this: our worst days are sometimes the best days for others.

"I Have A Dream!"

The "I have a dream" portion of Dr. King's speech has been quoted, recited and debated over more than half a century, and still stands the test of time from a literary, historical and motivational standpoint. Many say Dr. King's dream hasn't been fulfilled while others will say he would be proud of the progress we've made. The answer to whether the dream has been fulfilled will always lie in the eye of the beholder. I personally believe that Dr. King's dream is alive and well in many areas of our great country. There will always be injustice and it's unrealistic to expect perfection from imperfect people in an imperfect world. We, as a people, need to dream so that we can teach others what they too can achieve! I never met Dr. King, but his legacy continues because of what he stood for. It is up to us to form our own legacy and I, for one, choose to live the dream.

Happy MLK DAY!

The Catchy Phrase

Recently the topic of fear has come up in many conversations, whether it be in-person conversations or posts on Facebook, from a multitude of people. I posted a little while ago that that FEAR can be the abbreviation for: False Expectations Appearing Real. I then realized that, although this is a catchy phrase, it doesn't really help anyone dealing with the actual issue of fear. So, I decided to chime in with a thought. First of all, fear is a normal and healthy part of life. Fear becomes a problem when it is a NEGATIVE MOTIVATOR in our life. When a person is so fearful of everything that they become incapacitated, we need help them. Obtaining help is not a sign of weakness, as many would have us think. It's actually the opposite, since no person can exist without the help of others. As my earlier entry stated, we have choices when dealing with fear. You can run from them or face them the choice is yours. I am making a declaration to face my fears and, if I can't deal with them by myself, I hope some of you will stand by my side. And if you don't, I know God will be by my side regardless. So, what do I have to FEAR? Just sharing. Have a great day.

Holidays: The Real Meaning

As I prepared for church one Sunday, I realized that the reason so many people struggle around Thanksgiving and Christmas is because we have forgotten the real meaning of these holidays. We have taken the THANKS out of thanksgiving, and the Christ out Christmas.! We replaced these days with turkey and Santa and expensive gifts. I'm not opposed to eating and drinking, nor am I am bothered by the exchanging of gifts but when we, as a nation, forget the real meaning of these days and become greedy, selfish and disrespectful to others, we need to look at ourselves as ask what are we doing? Most Americans get to eat every day while people in other countries may not know where their next meal is coming from. My challenge to you all and myself is to be thankful every day and remember who the reason is for the season.

Friends 'n Family!

As I sit down to write this, I'm filled with so many emotions that I can't explain. As a child, I never looked forward to the holidays due to the struggles I was dealing with. I wasn't part of a close-knit family that got together with lots of laughter. There always seemed to be some type of drama and I didn't actually feel loved. I sometimes felt like I was an orphan. As I got older, two things happened that changed my life. The first was that I came to know Jesus as my Lord and Savior. Knowing the Lord taught me true love and I was no longer an orphan because he had given me a new family. The second event that had a great impact on my world was marrying my beautiful wife, Annabelle Noyola. She taught me how to enjoy family gatherings and to be a good host. Her giving spirit and cooking brought a lot of friends into our lives. I am thankful for the fact that today I can say my life is complete! I was super blessed to be part of a great event today by taking two families Thanksgiving dinners with my daughter, Alexis Daneé Clark, and her friend, Reshana Watson; also known as my other child. I also played basketball with my son, Isaac Clark and then enjoyed a house full of family, friends and lots of food !! I will close by saying, I am thankful that God chose to allow me some tough times, so that I could really appreciate the great times. Happy Thanksgiving to you all !!

Trials?

I was thinking about the many blessings I've had in my life and came across a Bible scripture that said, I should rejoice when I face trials, since they make me stronger. (I paraphrased this for all of you Bible scholars out there.) So, I want to say that I am thankful for the many trials I faced throughout my life because they've made me the person I am today. (You can decide if you like me or not, lol.) But I do believe that trials will help people build character.

We Need To Remember

December 1, 1955 was the unofficial start of the Civil Rights Movement, here in America. On that day, Rosa Parks was arrested for refusing to give up her seat on the bus to a white person. Sadly, the mentality of many people during that time supported her arrest, because they didn't feel she deserved to sit in a seat she paid for. Unfortunately, that type of division is crippling our country today. What makes it even worse today is that with all our technological advances, many people still don't know how to treat people. Poor race relations, elitism and selfishness have caused a great country to become stagnant in its growth. Many people turned a blind eye to injustice and have chosen to stay silent because they are more afraid of offending people than they are of doing the right thing. In the long run, the silent majority will always lose to the loud minority. If we truly want to be great again, then we need to step up and be the voice of the oppressed and offended.

God's Waiting Room

If you're like me, you hate to sit in the waiting room. However, the waiting room of God is different than other waiting rooms. The waiting room of God is actually a place of service--not waiting. When we are in God's waiting room, we should be waiting on God and om others. Our mentality has to be like a waiter or waitress in the best restaurant, knowing that our service will get us the best reward. When we DECIDE to serve in the waiting room, as opposed to complaining about how long it's taking for us to get what we want, we will have more peace and joy.

December 7, 1941

December 7, 1941 is a day that our country will never forget. It was the September 11 of that generation, and the people who fought for us were considered members of The Greatest Generation. Today is Pearl Harbor Day, and unfortunately many of those veterans have passed away, but I believe that this day is another opportunity for us to remember that FREEDOM is never free, and there are many people who sacrificed their life and well-being for the things we enjoy, and often take for granted. If you know a Pearl Harbor veteran, please thank them. If you know a veteran of the military, thank them. And, if you are able to read this without fear of harm, be thankful, because not every person in this world is BLESSED enough to live in a country that gives them the freedoms we enjoy.

The Forgotten

As I think about the many blessings in my life, I would be remiss if I didn't take time to share about the less fortunate. Although many of us will be able to spend time with family and friends during the holiday season, there is a large segment of our society who won't have that luxury. They aren't all homeless or unemployed. Many of these people are new to cities where they don't know anyone. Some are away from their families due to financial challenges and a variety of other reasons. This is the time for all of us to step up and make a difference. If you have the ability to invite someone else to your home, please do so. If you can't invite anyone over, try taking time to show kindness and have a conversation with someone new. Your kindness can make a difference to someone that is lonely and hurting! Trust me, I know from experience. I have been on both sides and I am thankful for those families who offered me compassion through the years, especially during the holidays!

Acceptance

Acceptance is one of the most challenging, yet freeing things a person can do in their life. Often times, people don't want to accept things about other people. This past October, a friend reminded me that acceptance needs to be applied to ourselves as well. He reminded me that I need to stop dwelling on my flaws and shortcomings and to just accept them, while I continue to work on myself. He also reminded me that I need to ACCEPT God's grace and mercy to help me overcome my challenges. That lesson is something we all need to hear. Stop beating yourself up, none of us are perfect! Accept God's grace and mercy and learn to enjoy the journey. Remember, if God can forgive you, then you need to forgive yourself!

Prayer

Prayer is the most powerful tool in our spiritual battle. A poor prayer life can lead to bad decisions and unfortunate circumstances. As Christians, we are told to pray continually, which means we need to have an attitude of prayer at all times. We also need to keep in mind that prayer is not just for us. If we are only praying for our own needs and forget about others, then we are being selfish. Often times people say they don't know what or how to pray. However, a person who really wants to pray will find that there are many things to pray about. I would recommend that you start by thanking God for your blessings, and then start praying for your needs and the needs of others. There are a lot of people who need our prayers. Let's increase our prayer time and see what God does!

Kindness

While I was traveling in Southern California the other day, I decided to have dinner at Panda Express. When I walked into the restaurant, I greeted the person who would eventually help me. After exchanging the usual pleasantries, we started to have a conversation. She shared with me that she had been at that location for two years, and with the company around ten years. As she put my order together, I noticed her hands looked like she may have had some arthritis and may have been in some pain. However, her smile radiated in the restaurant. As she completed my order, she thanked me and said she likes serving customers like me because I was nice to her. Her statement made me smile on the outside and hurt on the inside. I was glad that I made her day! But I was saddened that society has gotten to the point that we have forgotten what kindness toward others is really about. It doesn't take much to treat a person like we would want to be treated. Let's do our best to do better toward others!

Focus

What's your focus? When I was younger, I loved playing sports. I played three sports in high school and for a year, I played two sports in college. My passion for sports was very strong. However, I didn't accomplish my goals in sports. Although I played college basketball, I played at a junior college and then at a small school that is no longer around. I felt that my sports career was a failure. I say this to make a point. All too often in life we tend to focus on our failures and shortcomings instead of our successes and accomplishments. People who may succeed in one area of life can fail miserably in another. If we only focus on our failures, we will never really see our successes. We must change our thinking if we ever want to get to the level where we find peace and joy in life! Let's stop thinking about our failures 'as failures' and start view them 'as opportunities' to learn and be redirected to better things!

Faith

The subject of faith has been on my heart for a while I'd like to share more on this. Many people believe the Christian faith walk is easy! On the contrary, the Christian journey is neither easy nor hard. It is what it is. For some, the walk is very easy, but for others it can be more challenging. The call of a Christian is not meant to be an escape from the challenges that accompany this life. Rather, the call of a Christian is toward all eternity. Many Christians with strong faith suffer hurt and heartache. In my lifetime, I've noticed people are bothered by two things. The first is: why do bad things happen to good people? The second is: they don't understand why God allows something to happen? Although I am not a theologian, I will try to give the short perspective on both. First of all, good and bad happen to all types of people because of the world that we live in. God has given us free will, and with that free will comes consequences. Keep in mind that Cain, of Genesis, killed his brother Abel when there were only four people in the world. The second challenge, which is simpler to explain, yet harder to understand is this: God never told us to understand! He told us to trust. I have never read in the Bible where God asks us to understand his plan for our lives. We, as a society, are the ones who desire understanding. I can personally say that I have dealt with much heartache and pain in many parts of my life. As a matter of fact, if I am honest with myself, I can say that this year I dealt with some very tough things. However, I have to make the DECISION to trust God in the valley, so that I can rejoice on the mountain top. There will always be questions on the faith journey! However, it's best to pray and search the word of God than to get discouraged and leave the road!

The First Hug From My Grandson

For those of you who really know my daughter, you know that she is not a big hugger. As a matter of fact, if I get a hug from her, it's usually accompanied by a response like ... 'I was falling and I needed you to keep from hitting the floor.' When I picked her and husband up from the airport, I was reluctant to hug her because I was still in a state of shock seeing her pregnant and I didn't want to physically hurt her, so I gave the two of them the customary 'short hug' that people give when they're greeting a distant acquaintance. Well, that Christmas Eve, I feel that I received an early Christmas gift, and I can't contain my joy any longer. As I was standing in the hallway, I felt someone hugging me from behind, so I turned around and saw that it was my daughter. I didn't know why she was holding on to me, so I asked her if she was falling--and she said no. Then, she informed me that my grandson, Jaden, wanted to give me a hug, and she felt the need to comply. (Mind you, Jaden was still in her tummy!) I had no words for this priceless moment, but I did have plenty of tears. I was overwhelmed with an unspeakable joy that my daughter/grandson wanted to hug me! However, I was filled with excitement knowing that in April, I will be holding the son of the little girl that I used to hold! If being a grandparent is nearly as good as the anticipation I'm experiencing, then the world may not be able to contain me!

The Real Meaning of Christmas

One of the best things about getting older is the knowledge you obtain along the way. When I was younger, Christmas as was all about the presents under the tree. I wanted them all for me because I was self-centered like most kids. But as I got older, I realized that Christmas is about the PRESENCE of the Lord in my house, and especially my life. I still enjoy seeing gifts under the tree. However, MY JOY now comes from **giving gifts,** because I was given the GREATEST GIFT of all, when God chose to give his son for me! I am thankful for the peace I have despite the storms I may encounter. As you sit down to prepare for your holiday season, please remember the reason for the season! Merry Christmas to you all!

The New Year

If you want to have a successful new year, then you will need to make some changes!
Here are some suggestions:

- Hold on to your faith, your family and your friends!

- Let go of your hurts, your hang-ups and anything else that's holding you back!

- Only you have the power to change you!

Your Purpose

At the beginning of the New Year, I oftentimes reflect on the past year and think about what I can do differently or better in the New Year. As I listen to all the tributes to those who passed away, it makes me think about the purpose of life. Our world is full of people who are self-absorbed and focused only on themselves. While I do believe that we're supposed to be self-sufficient, productive people in society, I also believe that we need to inspire, motivate and encourage others to get to the next level in life. Most of the people reading this won't be able to impact lives from a position of fame. However, I believe that you'll be able to impact someone near you. There have been numerous people who spoke to me at different times of my life that truly helped me grow as a person. My kids are always giving me a hard time about talking to everyone I meet, especially young people. My response to them is, I just might be the one who helps them, just like so many have helped me. I want to challenge anyone reading this to impact lives with your words and your lifestyle. You may never know the difference you've made in someone's life, but you will know that you made a difference by living your life the right way!

Closer To The Lord

As I sit and think about this past year, I must admit it had some of the same similarities as years past. I had major ups and downs, made new friends on cruises and airplanes and was given new opportunities to grow and expand as a person and professional. I experienced unspeakable joy and severe heartaches! But most importantly, I felt and saw the presence of the Lord in my life. My hope for everyone is that 2019 brings them closer to the Lord, and that their dreams come to pass. I hope to increase my prayer time and to be more involved in my communities, as well as taking advantage of the business opportunities coming my way. I hope you all have a great evening and are prepared for a great new year!

Only Love...

As I prepared for 2019, I thought I'd look back on 2018 and share the most important lesson I learned. The simple yet profound lesson was this.: acceptance is the key to minimizing my stress! There are many things in my world that I don't like or agree with! However, fighting worthless battles only hurts me. I will never be silent on causes that need a voice. However, I will not allow what another person does to impact me to the point where I am counterproductive. As I said before and will say again, acceptance doesn't mean agreement. But without acceptance, I won't be able to reach those I'm trying to influence. Hate doesn't move people in the right direction! Only love moves people into the right way!

The Dinner

After 4 days with my family of nonstop laughter, having a baby shower, celebrating Christmas, game-playing, which included the Bakersfield version of monopoly, the millennial version of Monopoly and UNO, we decided to go to dinner and celebrate the end of a successful holiday week and a successful year. As I sat at the table, I was quietly moved with emotions. I found myself sitting at a table with my TWO college-educated children, a college-educated, super-smart son-in-law, and my teacher/wife who married me when I was young and has decided to stay with me in my latter years as well. As we conversed, I couldn't help but think of the struggles we endured to get to this point in our lives. We left our families to move to a city where we knew very few people. We had overcome financial and emotional challenges and endured some heartaches along the way. However, through God's infinite wisdom, I was able to see one part of his plan completed. I've been given what I always longed for--a stable family life. We don't always agree with one another but we always love one another. As we completed dinner, I shared with them how proud I am of all of them. The other members of our family shared heartfelt words as well. As we left the restaurant, I realized that, whereas we went to dinner to feed our stomachs, we left with hearts overflowing with joy!

The Struggle

I've been reluctant to write this one, but after much thought and consideration, I feel it's important information and others need to hear it. In life we are going to have struggles! However, we must realize that we don't have to deal with our struggles alone. Personally speaking, I deal with anger, disappointment, jealously, failure and many other issues. They don't always consume me, but if I don't work hard to keep them in check, I could be overcome by the emotions associated with them. As I got older, some of these issues became more challenging to deal with, while others have gotten much easier. One of the most important things I have to remember is that, I don't have to walk through these issues alone. Sadly, many people, especially men, don't want to ask for help. Many women feel the same way. However, women tend to be more open to discussing their issues than men. I recently heard about a young man who committed suicide. I hadn't seen him since he was a child. However, for a person to be brought down by life so low that they committed suicide, indicates they were beyond hope. I want to encourage any and all of you reading this to seek help if you need it. Please don't allow your pride to cause you to do something that will cause your family heartache for the rest of their lives.

Who Are You?

As I reflect back on the years, I came to the realization that many people aren't happy with their lives because of the fact that they don't know who they are. Many people go through life trying to be like others. They try really hard to be like their friends, relatives or someone famous. What those people don't realize is that while they are pursuing the life and lifestyle of someone else, they are missing out on building their own legacy. I want to challenge all of you to figure out who you are, so that you can be completely fulfilled in your own life. Once you figure out who you are, please help someone else figure out who they are. By helping one another, we will be able to make sure that there are more happy people in our communities this year than there were last year!

Politics

As I sit here thinking about lots of things, I'm trying to figure out why people in one of the greatest countries in the world can't seem to get along. It appears that we've reverted back to the days of elementary school where friends became enemies because they didn't agree on something. The difference between those days in school and now is that, friends CHOOSE to stay enemies because they don't want to accept the fact that other people hold opinions different than their own. Our freedoms and diversity are what makes us different as a society. We are not required to agree, like or even respect other people's points of view. However, we will be better off if we learn to accept others for who they are. Nothing positive will ever come out of hatred or negativity! Only through love and compassion we will be able to promote positive change!

All

"Seek first the kingdom of God and his righteous, and all of these things will be given to you as well." (Matthew 6.33) For years this passage intrigued me because I didn't understand the context of the word 'all.' In today's consumer-driven, self-centered, me-first world. many people view that scripture as 'the genie in the bottle.' However, after much prayer and study, I found the truth of this passage was embedded in the portion that proceeds the word 'all.' When a person truly seeks God and his righteous, there is a 'heart-change' that causes a person who was previously driven by the desires of this world, to change their thinking and motivation. As a result of this changed heart and mind, the 'all' (which they at one time used to seek selfish things) becomes the 'all things' that God desires. Therefore, one's prayers are more likely to come to pass. If we don't understand the scripture in its proper context, we can be led astray by false teaching! Seek wisdom so that you can be wise!

What Are You Complaining About?

Although I try to maintain a positive attitude most of the time, by the end of 2018 and the first few weeks of 2019, I found myself in a sort of funk that I would describe as 'mild depression.' As I was recapping my 2018 and rejoicing over all the positive things that occurred, I found myself wondering if there was anything significant left for me to accomplish. My son and I graduated from college and my daughter married a great man, moved to Atlanta and announced that she'd soon have our first grandchild in April of 2019. For most people, these events would have been enough to keep them going for a while. However, since my brain is always looking for the next big thing, I found myself feeling lifeless and without purpose. Fortunately for me, the Lord came through once again by sending some people my way to share words of encouragement. My neighbor was first one to speak into my life. His words and timing were exactly what I needed to hear!

A few days later, I had the opportunity to speak to two of former college teammates. Their words were also encouraging and perfectly timed. Shortly thereafter, I received a message that one of my former college friends was diagnosed with cancer. The next day, one of my customers informed me that their spouse was diagnosed with cancer. I say all of this to make a point: we will all have challenges in our lives. However, if we DECIDE to look inside and count our blessings, most of us will realize that we really don't have anything to complain about.

Acceptance

A few days ago, I was speaking with an old friend of mine with whom I'd reconnected through Facebook. As we talked about a variety of things, I was struck by something they told me. They said, the reason they enjoy our friendship is because I accept them for who they are. Although I was happy to hear why my friend thought so highly of me, I must admit that I was, and am, bothered by that. More people don't share the attribute of accepting others for who they are. My perspective on this topic is simple. Jesus accepted people 'where they were' in life, whole or broken, and we must learn to do the same. We will never be able to reach people that we can't or don't accept. Jesus also reminded us that the person who gets to cast the first stone must be sinless. We need to keep in mind that accepting a person doesn't mean that we have to accept 'their behavior.' Since none of us are without sin, we must stop judging others who sin differently than us, and start loving people who are created in God's image! By changing the way we look at people, we will create positive change.

August 1963

August 1963 was an unusual day in the nation's capital. It was a day where 250,000 people from all walks of life marched on Washington to protest the injustices of the time. The crowd was filled with people from all races and religions who wanted to see this country make some changes to benefit all its citizens. A 34-year old pastor took the stage with a prepared speech hoping to motivate, inspire and encourage the multitude who made the trek to the nation's capital. As he came to a close, he realized that they weren't as inspired as he had hoped, so he began what could be called the greatest impromptu speech ever given.

Dr. Martin Luther King, Jr., Day

As I reflect on Martin Luther King on the eve this annual day, I'm filled with many of emotions. Most are positive, however, I must admit, some are somewhat sad. Many remember Dr. King for his "I Have A Dream" speech, but he actually gave over 450 speeches during his lifetime. Others remember him for his stance on African American issues, but his forum was civil rights for all people. Some say Dr. King would be disappointed if he were alive today. I would have to disagree with that opinion. When I look at today's USA, I see progress and opportunities that didn't exist prior to his crusade. I will be the first to admit that we still have a ways to go in some areas, but I am THANKFUL of where we are today, because where we were 60 years ago, was no fun for those who came before me. Things are much better today than they were when my parents and grandparents were born. I'm am asking that you all join me in celebrating the LIFE OF A MAN who was instrumental in shaping the country and quality of life for many people! Remember also that our dreams can change the world if we pursue them! Although honoring Dr. King once a year is a nice thing, we will truly honor him when we fulfill his dream every day!

Giving

A balanced life is a well-lived life. Society says we should give to receive, while God says, "Give, because you have received!" Here is a short list of reasons why and how we can give!

- Give compassion because you have been given compassion.

- Give kindness because you have been given kindness.

- Give love because you have been given love.

- Give a smile because you have been smiled upon.

- Give generosity because generosity has been given to you.

- Give time because you have been given time.

- Although this is a short list, everything on here is free and it is a simple way to make a difference.

What's In Your Heart?

While I was in prayer the other day, this thought occurred to me and I feel compelled to share. In the book of Psalms, David asked God to search his heart. I thought to myself, if King David could ask this question, then maybe I should ask the same. As I have thought and prayed about this over the last few days, I realized my heart needed to be cleansed of some shortcomings. Selfishness, pride and jealousy were my Big 3 issues. Sadly, there are some little ones to deal with as well. At first, I was very discouraged at these findings. However, the Lord quickly showed his love and mercy toward me with this simple message: He LOVES me despite my shortcomings! I was reminded of the fact that he came into this world to heal the brokenhearted and redeem us. I was also reminded of the fact that my past is in the past and I need to quit talking about it, because HE has already forgiven me. After dealing with this issue for a few days, I realized that my responsibility is to seek the Lord with my whole heart and to trust him completely. Then, everything will fall into place. As I close this, please don't be afraid to ask yourself what's in your heart? You may be surprised at what you find!

Parents

The older I get, the more I realize that watching parents age is very difficult. In many cases, our parents were our first heroes. Our parents were our doctors, nurses, teachers and friends. They were also our chauffeurs and security guards. Although parents are always older than the children, they never seem old until they 'get older.' Many people have good memories of their parents. Unfortunately, there are many who have poor memories of their parents. Regardless of the memories you have of your parents, I want to challenge you to try your best to spend quality time with them. If you don't live near them, try calling them. Regardless of whether your parent was good or bad, your existence started with them. If you currently have a great relationship with your parents, continue to build on it. If you don't, start TRYING today. Because once they are gone, they are gone--and the opportunity will never come again.

Colorblind

I often hear people say that they don't see color when they look at people. Although I believe this is a great attribute to have when it comes to judging people, I am not sure if it's the best way to 'look' at people. God created all of us differently. Our color is part of that difference. In essence, choosing to see color means we aren't seeing people for who they are in the sight of God. Like a rainbow, our mixture of colors is beautiful when looked at together. We are better as a society when we learn to embrace our differences and work together for the betterment of our world. Regardless of a person's skin color, they are a valuable and important part of God's master plan. As a society, if we learn to appreciate the skin colors of people and not judge them by color, we will be able to overcome many things.

Cherish The Moments

February 3, 2018 started off as a great day for me. I was invited to watch a Los Angeles Clippers game in the Bank of America Suites that included a buffet. Shortly after tipoff, my son's Washburn team started their game and I had brought along my iPad to watch him online as well. Early in the game, my son got a steal and took off for the routine lay-up. As he planted his feet to take off, something happened. He couldn't get back up. Within 5 minutes of me seeing the play, I received a call from him saying, "My college career is over. The doctors believe that I tore my patella tendon." As I listened to him cry on the phone, I tried to be strong and encourage him. However, my heart was breaking and I wanted cry as well. At that moment, I had a bunch of questions and no answers. As I drove home and listened to the Washburn post-game interview with the coach, the reality of my son's injury hit me hard, and I broke down and cried like a baby on the freeway. All the years of training, practice and games ended on a freak injury. He was a starter and key contributor on a first place team who had worked extremely hard to accomplish his goal. That moment taught me one very important life lesson: cherish the moments you have with people, because you never know when it will be the last.

Are You Speaking Their Language?

Imagine going to a foreign country and expecting to succeed without knowing the language. I'm sure you can imagine how unsuccessful a person would be. Unfortunately, that is how many marriages are. In America, approximately half of marriages end in divorce. As a person who's been married for over half of my life, I know that marriage isn't easy. However, I also realize that marriage is easier when two people are speaking the same language. Although that statement seems like common sense, it really isn't, and here's why: men and women speak different languages! The key to success is finding out what language your spouse speaks. In the book entitled, 'The Five Love Languages,' the author points out that generally speaking there are 5 languages people speak in their relationships. They are receiving gifts, quality time, words of affirmation, acts of service (devotion) and physical touch. If a person doesn't understand what their spouse wants, they may be doing the right thing to the wrong person. Learning the language of your spouse can be challenging. However, it's not impossible if a person is willing to humble themselves and ask the right questions. So, as Valentine's Day approaches, let's work on speaking the right language so that we can truly enjoy the day with our spouse.

What If...

As I matured, I've come to realize that these two words... What If... can either free you or imprison you! The problem with a 'what if' list is that it tends to stagnate personal growth because it causes a person to focus on what they could have done, as opposed to what they have done and could be doing. My 'what if' list is too long to mention and too painful to recap. For far too long, my 'what if' list controlled and angered me because I looked at it as a failure list, instead of a learning list. I've come to the realization that if a person learns from their shortcomings, they are better off after failing than never having tried. Once we change our perspective on the term 'what if' we will find more victories than defeats in our lives. How different will your life be if you DECIDE that you will allow the 'what if' to be a releaser of what you could be, instead of allowing the 'what ifs' to be the jail that keeps you from being all that you could be?

Despite Who You Are

As I got out of bed this morning, I was hit with this thought: God loves me despite myself. Unlike people, including myself, he doesn't hold my past against me. Despite my shortcomings, he always supports me. Despite what I have done to him, he still promises to supply my needs. The love of God doesn't make sense to the human mind. It makes no sense that the creator of heaven and earth would send his only child to die for people who don't have a desire to serve him. So, whenever you're feeling down and out, remember that God loves you despite who you are!

To My Grandson

Dear Jaden,

You haven't met me yet but I want to introduce myself to you because once you arrive, there will be a lot of people trying to spend time with you, and I won't be with you for a couple of weeks. I am your grandfather. I am your mother's father and I am really excited to meet you. Right now, you are beating up your mother's insides and she is ready for you to come out. I have dreamt of the day you'd be born. Although we weren't in a hurry for your parents to have children, once we heard about you, we haven't stopped talking about you. Your parents are really happy about you joining them. They already have your room prepared and it's pretty cool-looking. Since I live a long way from you, I won't be able to be there when you first get home. However, I promise to give you my full attention whenever I am with you. We will have fun together and you can come to me any time that you're upset with your parents. I just want you to know that I love you, and I'm excited about your arrival!

Love,
Your grandfather.

I Am Missing her

Last year on this day, I was in Riverside, California celebrating my grandmothers 101st birthday. Sadly, it was the last big event we had together. Due to her health, she was unable to attend my daughter's wedding in April and my graduation in May. However, she was so excited about our accomplishments and proud of the people we had become, that she couldn't help but brag about us to her friends. Years ago, I started sending her money for the amount of years that she attained. I used to joke with her that I would need to get a loan once she got over 100, and I'd be happy to continue paying her as long as she was alive. Well, today would have been her 102nd birthday. Although I have the 102 dollars that I would have sent her, I don't have the words to describe how much I miss her. The dignity, strength and courage that she showed during her lifetime, was an example that I can only hope to emulate. Although I'm saddened by her earthly passing, I'm excited that she gets to spend her first heavenly birthday with my grandfather. I will always love her, and remember her on her birthday!

Tears of Joy

Modern technology is an amazing thing but it can sometimes cause problems. While my daughter was carrying our first grandchild, we don't see each other often, so she Face-Timed me every morning. She said she went to the hospital the other day thinking 'it was time' so on her way the she Face-Timed me again to let me know it was a false alarm. As her husband drove the car, she had a contraction that almost brought me to tears. As her dad, I hurt because my baby was in pain. She recovered and continued with her day. I called her that evening and asked her not to Face-Time me again until after her child was born, because it was too painful for me to watch her suffer. That next Tuesday, early in the morning, my son-in-law texted us that they were on their way back to the hospital--and this time it was for real. Later that morning, I got a Face-Time call and I was able to see the face of my beautiful daughter holding her beautiful, new baby son--Jaden Lamar Maynor!

Good Friday

When I was younger, I wondered why Good Friday was called Good Friday. After all, Good Friday celebrated the death of Jesus. I couldn't understand how people could celebrate such a horrible event. No one in their right mind would ever celebrate someone's death, especially such a gruesome one! However, after I gave my life to the Lord, I realized that Good Friday celebrating Jesus's death was the BEGINNING of life for the all of us, not the end, like so many had thought. The irony about Good Friday is that, the good Lord died for bad people! According to the Bible, we have all fallen short and there are none that are righteous outside of Jesus. Now, I see Good Friday as a truly good day for me because the Lord DECIDED I was worth the sacrifice. Understanding the meaning of Good Friday is crucial for any Christian because, once you know the truth about what the Lord has done for you, you will be able to celebrate how great Good Friday really is.

Are You Counting Your Blessings?

While I was having a conversation with a friend the other day, he said something that has really stuck with me. He said that I am really blessed! Although I often say that I am blessed, I had to ask myself, "Do I really count my blessings? Or are they just words?" Unfortunately, I must admit that often times I use the word blessed without thinking about its true meaning. According to Webster's Dictionary, one definition of the word 'blessings' means: "a thing conducive to happiness or welfare." Sadly, in our world today we are so focused on comparing what we have to others, that we forget to count our own blessings. I want to challenge others as well as myself, to really start counting the blessings we have. By counting our blessings, we will find that we'll will be happier and more able to share our happiness with others!

Trials and Troubles

The other day I was reading Psalms 22:1 and the first verse says, "My God, my God, why have you forsaken me?" My first thought was . . . I can relate to that. This scripture reminded me of the fact that there are many times when we cry out to God and feel that he doesn't hear us. After some soul searching, I realized that God always hears us! However, he doesn't always respond to us when or how we want him to respond. The word tells us in James that the testing of our faith leads to perseverance, and perseverance leads to maturity. No one wants to go through trials. However, if we are able to stand on the word of God and obey, God will reward us. Keep in mind that Jesus asked God to take away the burden of the cross, yet he finished the prayer by saying, "Not my will, but thy will be done." He was rewarded for his obedience, as we also will be for ours. Now it's our turn to stand firm!

It's Okay To Be Vulnerable

Over the last few days I've been filled with a lot emotions. My Sunday started at church with a message that I felt was directed at me. After I got home, I decided to watch a Motown special about Aretha Franklin who happened to be born the same year as my mother, which immediately caused me to think about my mom and the few memories that I had of her. As I was finishing my Aretha viewing, I got a text from my daughter about Kobe Bryant. I was shocked...in disbelief! My daughter is a diehard Kobe fan. Immediately after hearing about the tragedy, I was overcome with emotions. Although I was saddened about the loss of Kobe, my first thought went to his wife, who had just lost a DAUGHTER and husband! As more details emerged, I my thoughts turned to the other families and their losses as well. After processing the horrendous losses of life, I started thinking about my own family, especially my daughter because of her affection toward Kobe--and my dear father who had just recently passed away. I finally broke down and cried.

Although I didn't know what caused my breakdown, a friend of mine reminded me that it was okay for me to be vulnerable. She reminded that the passing of my dad coupled with everything else, had finally caught up with me. At that moment, I realized that it's okay to be vulnerable and to cry. We are human beings with emotions and those emotions are to be used. The next time you're overwhelmed with life, remember that it's okay for you to be vulnerable. Let it out and get help if you need it!

Tragedy

For anyone who watches the news on a regular basis, they realize that tragedies like the one that killed Kobe Bryant happen regularly. The fame and popularity of people will dictate the level of grief that society will demonstrate. The loss of life to anyone is devastating to their family and friends. As a person who lost their mother at age 7, I can't stop thinking about all the families impacted by the unfortunate event of Kobe Bryant's helicopter crash. There's a wife who lost her husband and child. There's a husband who had to tell his children that their mother won't be coming home. There is also a child who lost her parents and sister as a result of this accident. I'm sure there are many other stories associated with the nine people who perished that Sunday morning. As a society, we must understand that ALL these lives were important. However, Kobe and his daughter are the first names mentioned because they were the most popular, but not the most important! Let's continue to support all that were impacted and remember that life is short. We need to enjoy it with those that we love!

Blended Families

Although I will never claim to be an expert on this or most other marital topics, I will try to speak from the experiences I've seen and observed. With the divorce rate in America around 50%, it's very likely that a second marriage will create a blended family. In my opinion, a blended family can be just as good or bad as a non-blended family. The success or failure of a blended family will be determined by the amount of effort the parents and CHILDREN put into the new marital relationship. All parties need to understand that there will be challenges and obstacles ahead of them. However, communication, teamwork and compromise will give this new relationship an opportunity to succeed. Unfortunately, rushing into another marriage without proper time can cause problems from the beginning that are difficult to overcome. I strongly believe that people need to make sure that they are emotionally whole, prior to joining another family. After my mother passed away, my father's new wife already had four children of her own.

Her family was different from ours and we never really became unified. I have also seen the opposite--blended families that are so close you'd assume they were are all blood-related. Regardless of whether a marriage is blended or not, it's important to remember that successful marriages take work. One last thing to remember when it comes to blended families: step-parents are parents who chose to step up and be involved in the lives of children that weren't birthed to them. It takes a lot to fill that role. Make sure that respect is taught to the children.

The Martin Luther King Assassination

On April 4th 1968, a nonviolent man with a dream was gunned down because he wanted to see a better world for everyone! I am sure that there were many who applauded his death. However, I believe that the vast majority of society was devastated. Dr. King wasn't an ordinary person. He was a true leader and visionary. He wanted better for others and took action. He was arrested, beaten and ridiculed just because he sought equality for all mankind. His flaws have been well documented, yet his leadership cannot be questioned. He brought people together from all races to enact the badly needed changes. When he was killed, many people lost hope for a brighter future. However, his leadership was so strong that his dream lived on and still lives today! I don't believe that we have yet reached the mountain top. However, I do believe that we are closer than we would have been, had Dr. Martin Luther King never come along. Let's remember his life and not mourn his death!

It's Okay To Compliment Her

When men first start dating their spouse/significant other, they tend to be very complimentary. However, in many relationships, once the woman says yes and the ring is on, the compliments seem to stop. In some relationships you'd think that negativity was part of their wedding vows. I've learned from experience that a compliment goes a long way in maintaining and strengthening the marriage. As a teacher, my wife puts in long hours at the school where she works, and she can be overwhelmed with the responsibility of taking care of students and managing her classroom. She's now back in her classroom getting it ready for the upcoming school year, so I decided to call her. I could sense that she was tired when she answered the phone. When she asked me why I called, I told her I just wanted to tell her that I loved and appreciated her for what she does for me. Her tone immediately changed, and she joyfully said 'thank you.' It didn't hurt me to compliment her. However, the happiness I heard in her voice was priceless!

Remember Why

Long and successful marriages don't just happen. They are the result of two people dedicated to one another despite the obstacles they face. Sadly, people who've been married a long time start to forget about what they have, and instead tend to focus on things that they don't have. Often times, these thoughts can lead to feelings of discontentment and lead the parties down a road that ultimately ends in divorce. Although I don't claim to be an expert on solving the mystery of discontentment, I will say that after almost 30 years of being married, I learned a few things along the way. I truly believe that if a person who is challenged in their views about their spouse, would remember why they married them in the first place, they could start to rekindle the fire. Think about the happiness you've experienced! Think about the obstacles you've overcome together. Think about why you asked that person to be your bride or husband, and why you accepted their offer of marriage. Although understanding your 'why' may not solve all your challenges, it may prohibit you from making an emotional decision that could severely impact your life. So that next time you're going through a rough patch in your marriage, take a moment to remember your 'why.'

Your Children Need You

Since both of my children live in different states, I don't get to see them as often as I'd like. However, I've learned an important lesson that every parent needs to understand. Your children need you. I can't count how many times I have gotten phone calls or texts from my children asking for advice or needing an ear to just listen to them. Although parenting adult children can be challenging, the reality is that parents need to understand . . . we are parents for life! I believe that doctors need to tell every parent that they are parents until death does them part, because our children need us. One last thing to remember is that, if your children are reaching out to you, it means you've been a great parent! Children don't reach out to bad parents! Now go and enjoy your life sentence!

Fame

As I continue to process the tragic event of Kobe Bryant's helicopter crash, I like many others, am saddened. As a Lakers fan who watched Kobe grow up, I felt like I knew him personally. As a parent, the loss of his daughter has got me messed up, emotionally. His fame has the world mourning. However, it's important that we remember the "others" who perished as well. There were other sons, daughters, parents and siblings that were lost yesterday. Although none of them had the fame and notoriety of Kobe, they were just as important to their families and they deserve our prayers and support!

Flaws

As I scroll through my social media pages, I'm not surprised about the love and admiration Kobe Bryant is receiving. Sadly, there are those who will take this time to talk about his flaws, which are well-documented. Kobe Bryant, like many other celebrities was flawed! His greatness on the court brought about notoriety that most people will never understand. His celebrity also magnified his shortcomings! Today should be a day of remembrance, not a day of bashing him for his flaws! Remember that, Jesus never bashes us for our flaws. Before we bash him for his shortcomings, let's ask ourselves how we'd want to be treated if our flaws were made public!

Generations

For those of you who have been my friends on Facebook for a while, you know that I tend to post Black History facts during the month of February, and this year will be no different. As always, there will be a variety of people that are highlighted during the month. However, this year, in addition to the multitude of famous and influential, African American pioneers, leaders, innovators, justice activists and celebrities and many others, I plan to sprinkle in some knowledge about the generation that set the stage for where we are today: The Civil Rights Generation. American history has always applauded the accomplishments of the World War 2 Generation. But it's also crucially important that the accomplishments of the Civil Rights Generation are told as well. The greatest generation in Black History, as they are affectionately known today in the American Black Community, should also be acknowledged for their heroic efforts on the battlefield against the enemy—institutional racism! However, it's also important that we recognize the courage of many Americans, both Black and white, demonstrated during the Civil Rights Era. The main difference between the two groups is that one group fought against a foreign enemy to maintain our freedoms as a country, while the other group fought amongst themselves to gain equality for all.

You Are Important!

Over the last couple of weeks, the world has lost some legendary people in Kobe Bryant and Kirk Douglas. Both of these people had millions of fans and supporters throughout their lifetimes. They were both known worldwide and their passing caused ripples in the world of sports and entertainment. Sadly, our world has created a culture that values celebrities over "other" people. It's important that you realize you are important as well! A person's value or importance doesn't increase because of their popularity. Regardless of whether a person is a baby, senior citizen or anyone in between, they are important to their family and friends. We must be careful not to fall into the trap of comparing ourselves to others. Popularity will never equal importance.

Little Things Matter

Strong relationships understand the concept that little things matter. My wife and I tend to go to bed at different times. She is the early to bed, early to rise type person. While I tend to stay up later to get caught up on my TV or reading from the day. My bedtime is her security time. No matter how long she has been asleep, she seems to know when I crawl into bed. As soon as my head hits the pillow, she grabs my hand and holds it until I turn over. Due to my sleeping challenges I tend to toss and turn a lot. However, I make sure that I stay in a set position for a while so that she knows I'm by her side. Holding her hand for a few minutes doesn't cost me anything! However, the peace that she gets by knowing I'm by her side is priceless. Every relationship needs big things. However, it's important to understand that little things matter too, and they usually don't cost a lot!

Something To Think About:

For Women!

Since I've been a man for quite some time, I thought I would share a perspective that many women may not understand. Men are simple people with simple needs! However, our society has made men seem like they are more difficult than they really are. Although there are outliers in every group, generally speaking, the key to having a happy man is to treat him with respect and to acknowledge his accomplishments. Sadly, our society has focused so much on teaching independence and uniqueness, that they forgot to teach the simple concept of respect for one another, especially when it involves men. The women's lib movement of the 60's taught many women to disrespect men, which led to other challenges in our society. I strongly believe that a woman who treats her man with respect will get more from him because he will feel valued in the relationship.

Missing Someone

As I sit at my desk this morning, I feel that I must request prayer for those who are having their first Christmas without a loved one. I know from firsthand experience the pain of trying to celebrate without someone who made your Holidays special, is very hard. Sadly, I personally know of several families who lost someone this year. Although they may have a happy face, that doesn't mean they won't have moments of sadness because they will, in fact, miss their family members.

You Can't Blame Yourself

Recently, I've had several conversations with parents who are beating themselves up for the decisions their children have made. Although I understand their dilemma from personal experience, I have to admit that in recent years I've learned, generally speaking, parents aren't responsible for the actions of their children. If a parent taught their children right from wrong and the child chooses to make a wrong decision, it's not the parents' fault. Sadly, society will attempt to guilt parents into believing that they are the reason their child chose a wrong path. However, as a parent, you must understand that your children, just like us before we became parents, made decisions that may not have pleased our parents. It is natural to have concerns about your children's behavior. However, it's very unhealthy to blame yourself for anyone else's actions. So, the next time your child does something you don't agree with, remember, if they are capable of making a decision, they need to be responsible for the consequences--not you!

Communication:
Is More Than Just Words

Recently, while I was counseling a couple and the husband said something so profound, it blew me away. He said, "My wife communicates all the time, but I don't because I'm very quiet." Although I understood what he meant, he, like many others, don't understand the fact that communication is more than words. I have learned, and am still learning, that communication involves many layers. Your voice, your body language, your words and actions are all parts of the communication process. Regardless of the relationship, it's important to understand that effective communicators use more than words. Your words mean nothing if they are used with the wrong tone and body language. Consequently, you won't need to use many words to communicate if your actions are speaking for you. I often share with people that communication isn't what is said--it's what is heard and understood by the other party. If you want to be a good communicator, make sure that what want to say is being heard.

Not Everyone Is Happy

Although the holiday season is an awesome time to spend with family and friends, we must take time to remember that not everyone is happy this time of the year. Sadly, there are people who are grieving due to the loss of loved ones. Some, like myself, may be going through their first holiday season without their loved ones. While others may be dealing with loneliness and isolation due to family squabbles, finances or a variety of other reason. We should strive to put a smile on the face of others by being extra kind. A little generosity and compassion during this time of the year can go a long way in making a challenging time a little bit more tolerable. Let's treat others the way we would want to be treated if the tables were turned.

I Don't Understand!

As I sit here today I'm filled with lots of emotions. Since Thanksgiving, I've heard of at least two people passing away, and one of them was only 24 years old. Christians are no different than other people. We have our ups and downs. We go through trials and tribulations, and if we are honest with ourselves, we will admit that we question God and his will. Contrary to what some think, all these feelings and emotions are normal. Questioning things that are going on in our lives is going to happen. The Bible never tells us to understand! However, it tells us to trust God and his plan. Jeremiah 29:11: "For I know the plans I have for you," declares the LORD, "plans to prosper you and not to harm you, plans to give you hope and a future." I want to encourage anyone that may be struggling with their faith and wondering what God is doing, to hold on and trust him. I don't know his will or his plan for anyone's life, including mine. However, I do know that he is the only one with a perfect track record. So, let's hold each other up in prayer and encourage one another so that we can get through this journey!

HATE !!

I HATE HATE!! Unless the hate is toward something that is an injustice, hate is wrong and shouldn't be tolerated! Lives are damaged every day because of HATE! How much could be accomplished if our hate for wrongs and injustice were turned into love and action!

What If I'm Wrong?

Recently, I have seen more attacks on Christianity than I can remember in my lifetime. The attacks have ranged from Christianity being called a white person's religion, to people being killed just because they call Jesus their savior. I am not going to try to change anyone's mind. However, after giving this issue much thought, I feel that I should share my perspective. As a Christian, if I am/was wrong, I have lost nothing. I would have lived a moral life that demonstrated compassion for people, passion for life, supported people and organizations with my time and finances, and I will die with a good reputation. People won't have to lie at my funeral and say a bunch of things that weren't true to make my family feel good. However, if I am right, I still will have done the above-mentioned things, yet when I leave this body, I will be assured of my eternal home with my Lord and savior Jesus Christ. I will never get upset with someone who thinks differently than me. I just hope that they are right.

It Starts With Us

The recent mass shootings have made me ask myself one question: how did we get here? The vast majority of issues that we're dealing with started with us. ALL of us must look in our mirrors and ask ourselves how did we allow our country to become this way? As a society, we have allowed the loud minority to overtake the silent majority. We are seeing the results of our LACK of labor! We have become a society that is quick to judge others, and slow to do anything. The silent majority sat back and watched things happen because they didn't want to get involved. While the loud minority has taken over. You can pick any topic and hear the voices of the loud minority, while the silent majority says nothing. Parents stopped being parents because they wanted their kids to like them. We started giving participation trophies, instead of discipline. We blame, instead of taking responsibility. We give labels to fit the narrative, instead of speaking the truth. We are getting what we allowed. Our selfishness has led to a society of selfish people, that doesn't care about anything outside of themselves.

WE sacrificed conviction for convenience! If the topic is uncomfortable, we avoid it. Racism, gun control, mental illness, domestic terrorism, integrity and basic human decency should be discussed regularly. However, because everyone has become so quick to argue, instead of discussing it, then progress has been stifled. If we really want change, then it will start with us!

Prepared, But Not Ready

As I prepare for my dad's funeral this week I have learned some valuable lessons. I have learned that, because he planned well, the process has been relatively easy. However, I have also realized that just because I am prepared, doesn't mean that I am ready. Being prepared eases the stress for the family. Not having to depend on others for payments or donations is very comforting. However, losing a parent is a different type of hurt. And I can honestly say that I wasn't ready. Although I knew my dad was battling cancer, it seems that his demise was very fast. From diagnosis to death, it was less than three months. Losing a loved one is never easy! However, losing a parent is very challenging due their place in your life. Parents are your first protectors, providers, teachers and family historians amongst other things. They were your friends when you had no others, and they were your biggest cheerleaders. For those of you who still have parents and grandparents, please prepare for their passing. However, keep in mind that your preparedness will never make you ready.

Mad or Sad

I realized today that I will never see my dad on Earth again. Sadly, he passed away this morning as I was preparing to go and visit him. Recently, a friend of mine asked me how I feel about everything~~~if I was mad or sad. After pondering the question, I realized there are a lot of people who would be mad at the loss of their loved one. Although I am not happy about losing him, I am not mad at him, God or anyone else. I am not mad because I had a great relationship with my dad. We talked daily and toward the end, we talked a few times a day. I am also not mad because ... I am who I am ... because of the lessons learned from observing him. I am, however, extremely sad because I not only lost my dad, I lost a friend. He was the best listener in the world, which is really important for someone like me who, as you can tell, likes to talk a lot. His humility, work ethic and gentleness are all characteristics that were admiral to all, and I could do a better job of emulating! Please pray for those who lost loved ones as they go through the grieving process.

You Will Always Be Their Dad

Every time I start cleaning around my house I'm reminded of yet another memory. A couple of years ago, I found some pictures of my wife and I, before we got married, that brought me joy and laughter. Apparently, Facebook Nation wasn't a fan of my mustache. LOL. Last week's cleaning picture moved me to tears of sadness, joy and happiness. I was saddened because I saw pictures of two little people, our children, who are now all grown up! In fact, they are living independently in other states! Fortunately, I have many fond memories with them, whether it was sports or other activities. Although I can't get the time back, I am thankful that I was there, with and for them. I really miss those times when they were small and believed everything I told them. And I'm filled with joy because they turned out to be pretty darn good adults, who are enjoyable to be around--most of the time; LOL. My happiness comes from the fact that, although they are now "grownups" they still call and ask for advice. Because I am their dad!

They're Not Invisible

The increase of homelessness in our country is causing a large group of people to become invisible. I've observed a behavior by people that is sad and understandable at the same time. Although there is no easy answer to the problem, I'm confident that ignoring these people isn't one of the solutions. Every homeless person has a story. Sadly, their stories won't be heard by many because they are invisible to most of our society. If we want to see change, then we must be willing to engage those people that are different, and remember ... they are not invisible!

Acknowledgement

Women tend to be the unsung heroes in the world. Often times they do what needs to be done because it needs to be done. They don't wait to hear from others, they just do it. Although women are amazing, it is important for us, as men, to acknowledge what they do. Men, let's do a better job of acknowledging our wives and girlfriends and see how much happier they will be!

The Bible

As a Christian, I use the Bible as a guide to living a Godly life. However, I believe that using the Bible to justify bad behavior is wrong. It's important to realize that just because something is in the Bible, doesn't mean we should be doing it. The Bible is clear on what is right and wrong. It talks about many wrongs and the penalties for people who commit such wrongs. There many scriptures that explain what we should and shouldn't be doing. Justifying poor behavior just because it was mentioned in the Bible doesn't make it right. King David committed adultery and murder and paid the consequences. Although there is forgiveness for our sins and shortcomings, there are also penalties for our wrongs. The GRACE OF GOD was never intended to be used as a license to sin. As a Christian, if we want to see change, then we must properly apply the word of God for what it is--not what it isn't. If you don't agree with me, please read it for yourself.

True Service

As I processed the fact that my dad is no longer on this Earth, I can't help but think about the lessons I learned from him. One of the most important ones I learned from him was 'how to serve.' He served our country in the Korean War, but more importantly, he served his family. After my mother passed away, there were times that he worked up to three jobs. We weren't rich by any means. However, all our needs were met because my dad made sure that he ... served his family!

A Quiet Life

As I reflect on the past week, I realized a simple truth. A quiet life can have a positive impact on others. As I read again the tributes I wrote to my dad, I realized that his gift was his quiet demeanor. He didn't talk much and he had very few friends. Yet, the church was completely full at his funeral. Words like kind, caring and giving were mentioned often. My dad rarely raised his voice, even in anger he had a certain calm, soothing demeanor that demanded respect. Yet, he impacted many because his quiet nature made him a great listener. His forgiving nature, coupled with his... 'treat others like you want to be treated' policy... won over many! As I mature, I hope to emulate those qualities so that I too can impact others the way he impacted those he touched!

Marriage Advice

Someone recently asked me what is the best advice that I could give, regarding marriage. Although I'm not an expert, I feel that my 29 years of experience gives me a unique perspective to share from. Although the advice is simple, the application is the challenge. The success of your marriage will be determined by ... your decision to make it work! ... It's not always hard and it's rarely easy! However, when you become accepting of one another for who they are ... and aren't ... then you'll be a lot happier!

They All Grow Up

Facebook asked ... What's on my mind? ... and it got me thinking about a lot of things. With all the excitement about my grandson's birth, I realized that I hadn't shared another significant event in my life. As a parent, I have always felt that my job was to raise my children to be responsible adults. Often times, I've questioned decisions I made in the past. Sometimes, I felt like a failure as a parent, and other times I have felt like a superstar. Today is one of those days where I don't know how I feel. My second child, also known as my favorite son, decided to grow up. It seemed like it was only yesterday that I brought him home from the hospital. Today, he's a 23-year old college graduate who overcame more obstacles than most people will ever know or understand. Sadly for me, he decided to take his talent to Kansas City to start his career. Although I'm extremely happy that he had the intestinal fortitude to make such a big move on his own, I must admit that I'm a little sad that he's gone. I'm losing the basketball teammate who would pass me the ball to me, no matter how badly I played. I will miss having him around. However, I couldn't be prouder that the baby I brought home 23 years ago, is now all grown up!

True Beauty

I've been noticing recently that many of my friends share photos and videos of their aging parents and grandparents. Although some may say that it's in poor taste and degrading to show the elderly their weaker stage, I disagree with that assertion. I feel that these are images the world needs to see! As a society we are so focused on youth and beauty that we forget, true beauty is demonstrated in the love our elders showed us! Let's keep sharing those photos, and when we are privileged enough to see them, pray for those families whose elderly loved ones might also be in the last stages of life.

Happy Anniversary!
Dear Alexis, Jay and Baby Jaden:

Alexis, last year at this time I was nervous and excited to walk you down the aisle and give you away. The emotions I felt that day will never be repeated. (Part of those emotions were about losing my tax write off. LOL). And, as I handed you off to your husband, I asked him to take care of my daughter. Then, during your first year of marriage, I watched my little girl grow from a sometimes homesick young lady (mainly because she misses California food) to transforming into an amazing wife and mother.

Javonte (my daughter's husband), I'm so thankful that you're keeping your promise to take care of my daughter. You have not only provided for her physically, but you've helped her transition into her new role as happy wife and mother. Personally speaking, I am so THANKFUL for our relationship that words can't describe it. Whether we're talking sports, finance or any other subject, your wisdom, humility and desire to constantly learn and teach others is refreshing and encouraging!

And I love you dearly! I'm also thankful that we aren't just family, but also friends!

Baby Jaden, as your grandfather, words escape me as to how proud and happy I am to have you in our family! You've been in our lives for less than a month, and yet you've brought a joy to our family that words can't describe! I'm looking forward to spending more time with you in the future! I love you all!

Happy anniversary, my dear loved ones!

WHY?

That is a question we often ask when things don't go our way. Regardless of the situation, it's very easy to ask this question. Over the last few days, I asked this question more than ever. As a parent, I tend to internalize everything that happens to my children. When they succeed, I rejoice! When they hurt, I definitely hurt! Unfortunately, this is a time that I'm hurting big-time for my one of my children. As many of my Facebook followers saw that week, our worst fears were confirmed. My son, Isaac, suffered a season-ending injury that will cause him to have surgery this week. The recovery time will be long and hard! He will have to miss the last part of his senior year wherein he was a major part of a first place team. I'm not ashamed to admit that I cried a lot since I witnessed the injury that day. My only comfort is what the Bible tells me. "All things work together for the good of those that are called according to his purpose." I may still have questions about this, but for now, it's time to trust God and lean on him!

She "Needed" Gas

I rarely drive my wife's car because I hate having to adjust the seat and mirrors. However, the other day my wife mentioned to me that she was low on gas. Although I had just gotten home from the gym and didn't feel like going anywhere, I decided to take her car to Sam's club and fill it up. I'm sharing this story for one reason, which is ... our spouse's needs aren't always our wants. We must learn to be sensitive to their needs if we want to have marriages that are filled with joy and peace. Although it's nice to bring home flowers and candy to your spouse, sometimes it's better and wiser to fill up their car with gas. (Wink.) Taking time to understanding their needs will go a long way in keeping a marriage strong!

She Needs To Hear It.

Since I've been doing a lot of traveling lately I haven't been able to spend much time with my wife. Whenever I speak to her, I try to end every conversation with those three powerful words ... "I love you." The other day, my wife surprised me with her response. She said, "Thank you. I NEEDED to hear those words." As I listened to her, I realized something very important. She needs to hear it! As men, we get so busy doing stuff that we forget about our spouse's needs, while trying to provide for their wants. A spouse needs to HEAR words of love from our mouths as often as possible. Speaking loving words won't cost you anything. However, those loving words can go a long way in regards to your spouse's peace of mind and security in your marriage. Keep in mind that these principals apply to your children as well. Your words matter more than you know! Use them wisely and see how much better your results are in your homes.

Little Things Matter

I'm sure every married couple has some unwritten rules that cause strife when they aren't followed. My wife and I have one about making the bed. For the most part, the person who gets up last makes the bed. The other day I had to leave for a business trip and I was running late. Unfortunately, I was the last person out of bed so it was my responsibility to make the bed. After pondering how my wife would respond if I didn't make the bed, I decided that I had time to make it. I wasn't concerned about her being upset with me about not making the bed, I was concerned about her having to make the bed when she got home from her long day at work. We didn't get a chance to talk until late that evening. However, one of first things that she did was thank me for making the bed. Her gratefulness was a reminder that little things matter and the key to a successful marriage is doing the little things.

What Do You Fear?

Recently, I had a conversation with one of my friends about fear. The story that popped in my head was that of Elijah. You see, God had used Elijah to destroy many false prophets of Baal. Although Elijah had seen God do a great work, he was still afraid because he heard that Jezebel was out to kill him. The Elijah story got me to thinking about things that cause us to fear--and our response to those fears. Often times, we struggle with fear because we forget who we are serving. God is the ultimate deliverer. He is able to do exceedingly more than we can ask or hope for. Whether our fear involves family, work, or anything else, we must look to God as our deliverer and strength.

Finding Your Destination

While driving the other day, a thought occurred to me about childhood. When we were young, grownups often asked us what we want to be when we grow up, and we'd answer things like ... fireman, action hero, ballerina and princess. Once we grew up, many of us knew what we want and are determined to achieve our goals, no matter what the cost, while others (like me) had no clue and ended up finding their calling 'along the way.' The interesting thing about finding our life's calling is not the end result, but the journey that we took. I've been blessed to meet and get to know a variety of people. I've been around people who APPEAR to be successful and those that aren't. Everyone has to go on a journey to achieve their goals and dreams. The journey to your end result will have obstacles and challenges, and just when you think you've arrived at your destination, you will probably face additional challenges and obstacles that you didn't plan on. Successful people realize that the end result is not the reward. The reward comes from how you handled your trip.

How did you treat others along the way? What did you learn from your mistakes? What impact did you have on the lives of others? Were you thankful for those who helped you get to where you are today? Did you do the right thing despite the cost? When you can answer these questions, you'll be able to determine how successful you really are. Remember, our journey doesn't end until we expire, so be humble in all circumstances and keep pushing for your goals and dreams!

If He Were Alive...

Through the years I've heard people say that if Dr. King were alive, he would feel a certain way about things. I won't even attempt to give a perspective from his vantage point, however I will share a perspective from my viewpoint. Many people will tell you that the dream that Dr. King had is dead especially after the most recent presidential election. I will not minimize the value of the dream based on a politics. I will be the first to say that this country just like other countries has issues that need to be addressed. However, when the "I have a dream" speech was given many of those that were protesting were attacked, beaten and killed because they took a stance. Racial injustice was the norm and many people were treated terribly. Today people have opportunities that many of our ancestors couldn't even imagine. Minorities are succeeding in things that they weren't even considered capable of doing 50 years ago and in some people's minds not even 20 years ago. The greatest country in the world had BLACK PRESIDENT that was voted in by non-black people. I for one believe that the dream is alive and it's up to all of us to keep it alive for generations to come! Happy Birthday Dr. King and thank you for service!

You made a difference in my life!

Restoration

Often times when the word 'restoration' is used, it's usually in reference to homes or furniture. However, I want to share a perspective about restoration that is often overlooked, and that is in the area of relationships. Restoration of relationships can only come about when the parties involved DECIDE that the relationship matters more than the past hurt. Often pride and anger prohibit restoration. However, I have learned that for the most part there are very few reasons why restoration should not occur. Seeking forgiveness and understanding of the situation will help facilitate the process. Restoration is not only possible, but very healthy. I have heard many people say that they regret not reconciling with a friend or loved one after their passing. Don't be the person who CHOSE not to allow restoration to occur. Today is the day to start the process!

Privileges

Every year on the 4th of July people celebrate with a variety of activities. As I went to the store the other day, it hit me again that the reason we can celebrate is because our forefathers took a chance and risked their lives for us to have these freedoms. History hasn't told the whole story about all the sacrifices that were made. However, as an American I am free to go and do what I want to do without fear of harm. The privileges that I enjoy were not free since freedom is often gained by the shedding of blood and loss of life. The United States of America is not PERFECT by any means! However, I wouldn't trade being an American for anything. I want to wish you all safe and happy Independence Day and remember those that fought and those that are still fighting for all of us to live in this great country!

How will you be remembered?

As I wrote my grandmothers obituary, I realized some things. First of all, she was an amazing person who accomplished a lot despite many obstacles. Secondly, I didn't have to lie about her for the person that she was. Thirdly, I realized that I have a long way to go in my life to achieve the levels that my grandparents achieved in regards to impacting lives of their families and their communities. My new goal in life is to live my life so that my children won't have to lie at my funeral, and that the communities that I was part of will say that I made a difference.

Sometimes No ... Is Good.

I was just thinking that many times in our lives we get upset about things not going the way WE want them to go. I now realize that if I got everything I wanted, I probably wouldn't be where God wants me to be. So, I have a question for you all. Have you ever thought about thanking and praising God for the times that he said NO to you? If not, join me in doing so today!

Old School Gospel

As I sat at my desk today working on some things, I decided to listen to my old school mix of gospel music. It wasn't too long after I got started that I found myself in tears. My tears stemmed from joy and sadness. Joy, because I realize that God loves me and has my life under control even if when I can't see it. My tears of sadness come from the fact that there are so many people that are hurting and hopeless. I want to take a moment to share with anyone who is hurting to let them know that there is hope and help for anybody who will ask. Please don't allow pride to keep you from living the life that God desires for you. I may not understand your struggle, just like most people don't understand mine. However, there are people who want to help you overcome your obstacles. Stay strong and encouraged!

Police Brutality

I must admit I'm very angry about the events that are happening in our country. First of all, for a parent to lose a child is devastating. So, when a parent loses a child by the hand of those sworn to protect us, there can't be any words to explain the grief they must feel. When the Rodney King beating was caught on tape and the officers got off, I thought it couldn't get any worse. Well, obviously video and eyewitness testimony doesn't matter when it comes to the beating and killing of innocent people. It appears that if some people try to speak reasonably to police officers then it's considered a threat and a cause to get shot or beaten. The sad thing about everything that's happening is that, it's become so normal that it's barely making the news anymore! I am not indicting all law enforcement officers! I RESPECT THE BADGE AND THOSE WHO DO THE RIGHT THING! However, bad cops getting off because they are afraid when a person asks a question, or runs the other way and they feel the need to shoot them, needs to be stopped! PLEASE UNDERTSAND MY POINT OF VIEW HERE. I know that there are bad cops from all races! However, the vast majority of people getting killed are young Black men! As the father of a Black son and Black, future son in law, I must admit I have my concerns about their health and wellbeing. Please go back in time with me for a moment and understand what I need from you all. When Dr. Martin Luther King, Jr. started promoting change, he got people to help him. People of all races and backgrounds were committed to doing what needed to be done. I'm asking that we do it again. We need to do it again! If you need some motivation, ask yourself one simple question: how would you feel if it were your child being victimized? Let's make change happen!

It's Okay To Love And Trust Again

The other day I had a conversation with a friend about relationships. He shared with me that one of the challenges he sees with people in relationships is that when they come out of a bad one, they tend to treat the next person the same way the previous person treated them. That next day, driving in my car, I couldn't stop thinking about what my friend had said, because of the sheer truth of it. Although loving and trusting a person makes you vulnerable, that vulnerability is what makes you enjoy that person. No relationship can last riddled with doubt and insecurity. The obstacle most people need to overcome is--the past! Regardless of what another person has done to you, you should not hold it against the new person. Hurting people tend to hurt other people. Since men tend to hide their feelings, they harm others. My simple advice to any man or woman out there who may be hesitant to begin a new relationship is ... take it slow. Learn to love and appreciate yourself first so that you can be your best you in the next relationship.

The Civil Rights Act

Recently, I had the opportunity to visit the Civil Rights Museum in Memphis, Tennessee and I was fascinated by what I learned. On July 2, 1964, Martin Luther King and Robert Kennedy were on hand to witness the signing of the Civil Rights Act. It could be argued that this signing was the most significant event to address race relations since the Emancipation Proclamation. Some will say, change has been slow and race relations are no different than they were 60 years ago, while others say we've come a long way. Both sides can be debated and there would be no clear winner. However, the reality is that we are closer to Dr. King's dream than we were 60 years ago. Believing we can all live in a world where everyone will be treated equally is an unrealistic expectation. However, we must try! Change will only occur when people decide to work together for a common goal. In 1964 we saw a rainbow of people stand together for a common cause. Let's see what we can do today with all this technology, and continue to make the world a better place.

I Forgive You!

"I love you." These three, powerful words can change our homes, communities, country and our world. Healing can't begin without forgiveness! Many people are holding onto grudges for things that don't even involve them, but have been passed down from previous generations. Forgiveness isn't always easy, but it is always necessary. And I will be the first to admit that this is an area, I must work on daily. However, I have to come to realize that holding onto grudges and bitterness doesn't make us stronger. It makes us weaker. Let's start some new traditions of forgiveness and loving others. And, that includes those who have wronged us in the past. Being angry with someone doesn't hurt them. It hurts the person who is angry!

Dear Alexis ... aka ... Lex ... Boog:

In October 1992, your mother threw me a birthday party. On the cake she wrote 'Happy Birthday Dad!' Although I didn't know that ... you would be you ... I was excited to have a new edition to our household because we needed a tax write off. (LOL.) As I watched you grow into your own person over these last 24 years, I saw you go from a frog to a princess. (Inside joke!) Before you move on to your next phase of life, I wanted to tell how much I've enjoyed having you as my daughter! I enjoyed watching you sing and dance. I loved watching you compete in sports and I really enjoyed coaching your basketball teams! You may not have always won the competition, but ... *I always won!* ... because I got to see you do something you enjoyed and, most importantly, I was able to spend time with you. I will miss our weekly lunch dates, although my wallet and my waistline will be happier. I will also miss watching the Lakers with you, although FaceTime will make it possible from time to time. I will miss watching old school shows with you like *Cosby, A Different World* and *What's Happening*. I will miss your quirky sense of humor (although I won't miss you telling me how funny *you think you are*!) I want to congratulate you on your special day! In a few hours your name will change, in a few days your address will change and in a few months your tax status will change. (Sadly, my tax status will be changing as well). If you give your husband, Jay, half the joy you've given me in your first 24 years, then he will, indeed, be a very happy husband! Always know that your dad loves you!

Strong Marriages Are...

Why is marriage so hard? This is one of the easiest tough questions to answer. Marriage is hard because it involves two people who CHOOSE to join together and become one. However, those two people will always be two people. The challenge in marriage is--learn when to compromise and when to take a stand. Strong marriages are built on respect! No one person in the relationship is more important than the other. Strong marriages understand and embrace their roles in the relationship. The stay at home mom is no less valuable than the bread-earning dad. When married couples learn to appreciate their differences, many of their problems disappear. Successful marriages don't just happen! They take time, energy and a lot of patience. Learn to support and encourage each other's dreams and goals. Keep in mind that even if you do all the above, marriage will still be hard. However, it will be less hard and more fulfilling when you become one in mind!

How Do You feel?

Since my daughter was proposed to last year, I've been asked a question more times than I can count. "How do you feel?" After pondering the question, I now think I have the answer. I will admit that I'm dealing with a bunch of emotions. As the father of a daughter, I've always WANTED a few things for her: to be strong and educated. I wanted her to be able to reach for the stars and achieve her goals! I wanted her to have a strong relationship with Christ and to be called a good wife! Although I feel like all these 'wants' have been accomplished, the 'wife part' has been the hardest for me because that means I will no longer be the person she depends on. When she first started dating her fiancé, she told me that he was a lot like me. That gave me joy--and concern--because I know my flaws. However, as I watched their relationship grow, I saw the genuine love she had for him. The way she looked at him when they were together reminded me of the way I looked at my wife when we first met.

And, as I watched him, I saw that he treated her like a queen! So, to answer the question, I am and will always be very happy that my baby girl has been blessed with a good man and has found joy and happiness! I, on the other hand will be a little sad because I'm losing a tax write off. (I like saying this a lot because it's a dad thing!) In conclusion, her happiness is more important than taxes!

It's Not All About You

As I research Black History facts and grow as a person, I'm amazed about the things I'm learning about people, in general. Sadly, we've become a society that is so self-centered, they no longer want to help others unless it benefits them. No one person has impacted change by themselves. Every major change that occurred in our world has come about due to a group of people banding together to create the needed change. The Civil Rights Movement would not have occurred without the support of many white people as well, who decided to take a stand against the evil behavior of racism. A United group of people is very powerful! However, a selfish society is very destructive! Let's remember that and never forget. It's not all about you!

The Walk

Prior to me walking Alexis down the aisle, I had my last conversation with her as an unmarried person. I told her that I loved her and that if she would trust God, everything would be alright. She told me not to make her cry and fall down. As I started walking down the aisle with Alexis, my mind raced with many memories. In July 1994, Alexis started walking. She didn't start walking until she was about 13 months old. Although she was only 13 months, she needed to be the center of attention, and she started walking while we were at a friend's birthday party. The problem was that we were outside and she started toward the street!—and that's when she definitely got our attention. As Alexis and I continued our walk down the isle, my mind sped through memories of junior high, then high school and eventually college graduations. Then, I remembered her legs running on the soccer field, basketball court and the track. However, my most vivid memory was when she ran to the door to the hug me, when I came home from work. I should have appreciated those hugs more because she doesn't hug me anymore--not frantic like that, anyway. LOL.

As we approached the alter, I realized that my little girl was now a woman about to become a wife. When I responded to the pastor's question about who gives this person away, I could no longer contain my emotions! I cried, but not too much, because I promised her I wouldn't. Then, I turned to Jay, Alexis's soon-to-be husband and whispered, "Please take care of my baby girl." He reassured me that he would and, at that moment, I had the peace I needed to enjoy the rest of the ceremony. Our walk made me appreciate the sacrifices I made to be in her life mentally, physically and spiritually. Because memories will last forever.

The Dance

After witnessing the beautiful wedding ceremony between my daughter Alexis and her husband, Jay, and visiting with the many friends and family in attendance, Alexis and I finally had the chance to talk. The discussion took place during the Father-Daughter Dance. Her song choice of "Isn't She Lovely" by Stevie Wonder was perfect for the occasion and her personality. (She thinks very highly of herself. LOL) As we danced, I shared with her that no dad ever believes any man is good enough for his daughter. That's when she reminded me that Jay is a very good man and she loves him dearly! I then asked if she was happy, and she said, "Yes, very happy." So, I told her that I was happy because she found her dream man. I told her that all I ever wanted for her, was to be happy and live her life with a man she loves. She assured me that my goal for her had been realized. As we finished the dance, we hugged one more time, whereupon I told her that I loved her and bid her to enjoy her special night.

It was hard to let her go. I shed a tear of joy because I had played out this scene in my head over and over throughout years, and now it had finally come to pass. As I reflected on the weekend and the wedding, I realized that I am very blessed to have a daughter who chose a good man, one who reminds her of her dad. At the end of the night my wife and I flopped into bed. I turned to her and said, "We did it! We raised a great child who brought us another son for us to love!" She agreed and then we passed out. We're just not that young anymore!

The Legacy

During tough times I think we need to look back so that we can plan ahead. Although things have improved dramatically in today's economy, we all know that things are still tough for many people in our country. Many people lost their homes and jobs during the mortgage crisis between 2008 to 2014, but many are still hopeless, wondering what to do next. I recently spoke to a man who was around during the Depression Era of the late 1920s and I think his perspective will help us press forward during challenging times. I hope you enjoy his story.

His name is Thomas Hightower. He's a Black man born in the south in 1922. Thomas was a big man with a big voice but a gentle demeanor. He didn't have the opportunity to get much formal education due to his race and family situation. He left home at age 13 and worked odd jobs until the Second World War, whereupon he worked in the factories that made military supplies. He came to California in the early 1950's looking for an opportunity to live the American dream. I asked him how he overcame the obstacle he faced. Regarding racism he said, "One bad person doesn't define a whole group of people and there are good and bad people in all colors." In regards to his lack of education, he said he regretted not having more of a formal education, however, he was not going to let it keep him from 'becoming educated.' He found a "good" job at a junior college as a janitor where he worked for 27 years and was quick to remind me that he started at the bottom and finished at the top, as the Head of Maintenance. He also wanted me to know that he never missed a day of work in the 27 years! During his working years he was able to achieve the American dream of buying a home! Actually, he bought several homes throughout the years. His last home, which he bought prior to retiring was in the country, where he and his wife ran a little farm business. Like many others, Thomas faced adversity, including the loss of his only child—my mother. I asked him how he could stay so positive during the tough times he had faced, and he told he didn't have a choice. He said, "I could've whined and complained and lost all my friends, because even though people say care, they really don't want to hear about your problems." He continued, "Or, I could press on in life and make the best of what I did have." Regarding blaming others, he gave me some great advice. He said, "We may point a finger at others but we still have four fingers pointing back at us.

We must look to ourselves for solutions and not blame others for our problems, because the only person we can change is ourselves, and that," he said with a twinkle in his eye, "is a challenge in itself." Thomas wanted me to know one last thing before our conversation ended. He reminded me that if we are honest and hardworking, we will always have a job, but more importantly we will have the respect of our fellow man. "Respect, pays a lot more and lasts a lot longer than any job!"

Thomas Hightower was my grandfather. He passed away in 2008, and he left behind a legacy that I believe can inspire all of us to press on during these tough times.

What legacy will you leave behind?

God bless you on your journey through life.

Best regards,

Ed Clark

We hope you enjoyed the reflections and prose of Edward Clark. For additional copies of this book or to schedule a speaking engagement, feel free to contact Ed at the following:

Email: Edclark9082@yahoo.com

Facebook: ed.clark.7

LinkedIn: Ed Clark Bakersfield, CA

Made in the USA
Columbia, SC
01 April 2020